French and India

Bob Bearor

HERITAGE BOOKS
2007

HERITAGE BOOKS

AN IMPRINT OF HERITAGE BOOKS, INC.

Books, CDs, and more—Worldwide

For our listing of thousands of titles see our website
at
www.HeritageBooks.com

Published 2007 by
HERITAGE BOOKS, INC.
Publishing Division
65 East Main Street
Westminster, Maryland 21157-5026

Illustrations by Joe Lee

Photographs by Al Cederstrom

New maps by Bob Bearor

Old maps from the collections of the Fort Ticonderoga Museum

Other Heritage Books by Bob Bearor:

The Battle on Snowshoes

Leading by Example, Partisan Fighters & Leaders of New France, 1660-1760
Volumes One, Two and Three

International Standard Book Number: 978-0-7884-1475-6

This book is affectionately dedicated
to our sons and daughters,

Cliff and Ted, Becky and Jenny,

the twenty-first century equivalent of Canada's
fabulous family of LeMoynes.

Because of your dreams, schemes, and the amazing
accomplishments in your lives, your mom and I now know
how Charles and Catherine LeMoyne felt about their
Maccabean brood of heroes.

Contents

List of Illustrations and Maps vii
Foreword *by George C. Neumann* ix
Preface xi
Acknowledgments xv
Introduction xix
Prelude xxi

PART ONE: *The Battles*

Chapter 1: 1757 - Ambush in the Snow 1
Chapter 2: 1758 - The Bridge, the Brigadier and the Hill
.... 19

Centennial Poem, by Hon. Clayton H. Delano, 1864 36
"Ticonderoga" poem by Percy MacKay, 1909 37

PART TWO: *The Controversy*

Chapter 3: The Methods 41
The Trek 43
Drying the Muskets 45
Archeological Metal Detecting *by Keith Dolbeck* 49
Chapter 4: 1757 Site Location 55
Chapter 5: 1758 Site Location 63
Chapter 6: The Artifacts 73
The Last Page 93

Contributors 95
About the Author 99
Bibliography 101
Index 105

Maps, Illustrations and Photographs

Maps of Battlesite area

Map showing area of 1757 Ambushes (Map A) 3
"Sketch of the Country Round Tyconderoga" 26
Copy of a Map in the Possession of the Marquis of Sligo
    Sent Home by Captain Monypenny
    with the Report of Lord Howe's Death 28
Area of Battle in which Lord Howe was killed (Map B)
    67

Illustrations

Rangers prepare to ambush French sleighs xxiv
Officer of Les Compagnies Franches de la Marine 8
British Officer 18
Musket drying procedure 46
Shoes 75
Gaiters 76
Moccasins and liners 77
Ice Creepers 78

Photographs of Artifacts found at Battlesite

Shoe Buckles and Ice Creepers 72
Musket balls 83
Gun flints, Coins and Medals 87
Gun parts 88
Various accoutrements 89
Folding knife and blade 91
Tomahawk and Belt Axe 91

Other Photographs

Keith Dolbeck and Dan Blanchette 94
Bob Bearor and Greg Geiger 99

Foreword

A nation, as with an individual, eventually becomes what it understands and believes. Thus, while America is now occupied with a major technology transformation, it is also significant that we are undergoing a rejuvenation of historical interpretation that is revealing a far deeper and realistic appreciation of our early history.

One of these major factors is the emergence of many thousands of "reenactors" who recreate and dramatize with dedicated authenticity those prior generations who sacrificed so much to win and preserve our freedom. In doing so they are bringing to life much of our heretofore "faceless" academic interpretations of history to reach legions of young Americans who have been deprived of identification with our country's core values as a result of declining historical emphasis in most schools and families.

This latest work by Bob Bearor is an excellent example of how authentic reenactors can lead us to the solutions of key questions which have long eluded historians—in this case the actual locations of two dramatic events in the French and Indian War.

You will notice his disciplined methodology that begins with the research of the available contemporary records followed by a meticulous recreation and use of the clothing, weapons, equipment, and established period practices in the field. His final discovery of the probable site for both Rogers' 1757 First Battle on Snowshoes and the Death of Lord Howe in 1758 is then verified through the number and variety of artifacts recovered by Keith Dolbeck and Dan Blanchette using modern technology and techniques. Notice also that despite most professional archeologists' blanket disdain for so-called "diggers," these reenactors have followed a systematic disciplined examination of the area—suggesting the advantage of more future cooperation between both groups to achieve their common goals.

Bob Bearor has combined his deep love of North America's heritage with extensive real world research to create this easily read book. I highly recommend it as a thoroughly enjoyable and valuable contribution to our understanding of this critical period in the forming of our nation.

GEORGE C. NEUMANN
November 24, 1999

Preface

The tremendous success of my first book, *The Battle on Snowshoes*, took me quite by surprise. In fact, I was overwhelmed not only by its popularity within the historical community, but even more so by the enthusiastic response of the general public.

As time went on, I felt that the real satisfaction I gained from *The Battle on Snowshoes* came not from the amount of books sold, or the number of printings, but from the people I met because of it. People such as Fred and Carroll LaPann of Hague, New York; Dick and June Weller of Earlville, New York; Adirondack songwriter and singer, Chris Shaw, whose next album will feature the ballad "The Battle on Snowshoes"; Adirondack Mountain Club (ADK) Education Director, Anne Green and many, many others.

Since publication of the book, my wife, Holly, and I have traveled to seven states and Canada, and have done more than 50 book signings coupled with a half-hour slide presentation about the battle. I have spoken at libraries, museums, historical societies, Boy Scout banquets, senior citizens' meetings, and forts such as Ticonderoga, Niagara, William Henry, Edward, Ligonier, Necessity, Western, De Chartres, Number 4, and St. Helen's Island in Montreal, to name a few. These talks, in addition to the many letters I received and answered, allowed me to meet, talk with and genuinely get to know the people who read the book, and to find out what they liked about it.

In May of 1997 I was one of the guest speakers at the annual War College at Fort Ticonderoga. There I met such great authors and speakers as George Neumann, George Bray III, Robert Mulligan, Dr. Russell Bellico and others.

That very weekend, the idea for this book was born. As the War College ended, my friends, Fred Gowen and Greg Geiger, and I were winding down the hectic weekend with an 18th century brush camp in the mountains above Trout Brook Valley.

It was also on that same weekend that Fred, Greg and I had the immense good fortune of meeting Keith Dolbeck and Dan Blanchette, who, besides being incurable 18th century history buffs like ourselves, were amateur archeologists and metal detector enthusiasts. They proceeded to show us many of the artifacts they had obtained in this area, and our conversation naturally turned to the never-located sites of a different snowshoe battle involving Rogers' Rangers in January of 1757, and the battle in July of 1758 that resulted in the death of the celebrated Lord Howe. Although we all had our theories and feelings about these events, the locations had remained a mystery throughout the centuries.

From that day onward it became our goal to try to locate those places and share our findings with everyone.

First, we conducted extensive research using all books that contained any reference to the battles. We used all first- and second-person accounts, orderly books, diaries, letters and maps that fit the descriptions.

Next, I personally took the book research a step further by trekking out the routes in period clothing and equipment, in summer and winter (with snowshoes) to actually see the lay of the land and try to corroborate the times and distances as found in both the French and English journals.

Finally, after securing permission from the landowners, Keith and Dan scoured the various sites with metal detectors.

It wasn't long before the true battlesite was discovered. This book will tell that story to you.

History should not be boring or dull, or a rehashing of the same old stories. History should be educational, enlightening and enjoyable. This book is all that and more.

This book is also controversial. Not everyone who reads it will agree with our findings and statements. That is all right; differences of opinion make the world go round.

Hopefully, this book will not only bring satisfaction and knowledge to the reader, but it will also stimulate the mind and imagination to another level. It is my sincere wish that you will both learn from it and—most of all—enjoy it.

Bob Bearor
September 1999

Acknowledgments

As I stated in my first book, *The Battle on Snowshoes,* no man is an island, and no author ever successfully completed a book without the help of many people. This book is no exception.

First and foremost to my family. My wife Holly, sons Cliff and Ted, daughters Becky and Jenny. Thanks for your patience, understanding, and constant prodding to keep going and get it done.

That same encouragement came from my woods trekking partners, Fred Gowen, Greg Geiger, and Dan Broderick, who besides sharing campfire talks, debates, and knowledge, helped also by sharing much of the original source material found in this book.

In the acknowledgment section of *The Battle on Snowshoes,* my last credit was given to my close friend and editor, Roxanne Carlson. I said that Roxanne had taken a good book and made it better. That was an understatement.

Roxanne took the "diamond in the rough" and polished it into a brilliant gem. Everyone who has enjoyed *The Battle on Snowshoes* and this book also, should be aware of that.

Unless one is superbly gifted as a writer, and I do not consider myself as such, an editor like Roxanne is priceless. She has made these books concise, well worded, and enjoyable. I am very grateful for her help, expertise, and friendship.

Another very special lady, whom I owe a great deal of thanks, is Anita Dolbeck, sister-in-law of Keith. Anita has been a teacher in the Ticonderoga school system for almost 20 years. I was privileged to have her as my proof reader and typist. Her talents, personality, patience, and genuine good nature, made a hard task a joy to complete. Thank you, Anita.

Where would I be without the tremendous help, encouragement, and sharing of ideas, sources, and knowledge, from my esteemed friends and fellow writers such as Burt G. Loescher, George Bray, and George "Peskunck" Larrabee? I especially call attention to the word "sharing." It is because of the unselfishness and desire to help, that these men have provided us—you and me—with a new awareness and understanding of history.

A very special thank you goes to George C. Neumann, who not only wrote the wonderful and very moving foreword to this book, but who personally has been an inspiration to me as a writer and a public speaker. George is a mentor, not only for me, but for all those who love history, and the good and true values and heritage of this great nation of ours.

Special thanks go to the Lake George Historical Association, staffed by Grace MacDonald, and Marilyn and Mario Mazzeo. These fine people dedicate their time and efforts to help propagate history for Lake George. The Association building is located on Canada Street in Lake George village, and serves as a museum and bookstore, with tons of books and information available. I highly recommend it to those interested in early American history, especially that of Lake George.

Thanks go to the staff of Fort Ticonderoga for their help and the use of maps included in this book.

I would like to commend the Lake George Basin Land Conservancy, for its vital role in acquiring land, such as Rogers' Rock, and setting it aside for the use and pleasure of all. By their actions the public use of these historic sites is guaranteed. They have remembered the past and preserved and protected it for the future.

A very dear thanks goes to Stephanie Pell-Dechame, who was most gracious and helpful in allowing me to use the manuscript, "To Bite the Bullet," which was written and researched by her late husband, Roger Dechame. Roger shared his time and immense knowledge of the historic places of the Ticonderoga area battlesites and locations. In fact, Roger's theory of the site of the first Battle on Snowshoes turned out to be astoundingly close, only 1/4 mile away, and I only wish he could have the satisfaction of knowing that. He was a great friend.

To Al Cederstrom, my photographer, and Joe Lee, my illustrator, I owe my thanks for the high quality photos and drawings that enhance this book and make it so very special. Their work speaks for itself. Great job, guys!

To all the "gang" at Heritage Books, Inc., it has been a pleasure and a privilege to be part of such a fine company.

Finally. A special and heartfelt thanks goes to two fellows who are not only my mentors, historical buddies, and hunting partners, but great guys who I am privileged to call my dear friends, Fred LaPann and Dick Weller.

Introduction

The use of metal detectors to find and uncover historical sites and relics is controversial (to say the least), with the pros and cons from both sides being pretty much equal.

This book is not intended to be a statement condoning the use of metal detectors, nor is it to condemn them. I ask the reader to look upon the facts, as I have, with an open mind.

Historical places such as Fort Ticonderoga should be considered sacred grounds and strictly off limits to any kind of relic hunting. The removal of any artifacts, metal or otherwise, is wrong and indeed a crime.

Private property is another matter. The search for artifacts can and should be done, but only with the exclusive permission of the owner. There is no other acceptable way. This is the only way that Keith and Dan have operated.

In the town of Ticonderoga, as well as all over the United States, new homes, trailer parks, supermarkets and malls, fast food restaurants, etc., are constantly being built, reshaping the community and, unfortunately, closing the door to the past. Unless we take the opportunity to find and document the relics that lie in the path of development, one can only imagine how much is lost when graders, bulldozers, diggers, and landscapers remove hundreds of tons of soil and reshape the land.

Dan and Keith have documented and catalogued each artifact and its depth and location so that in the future people can know what was once found there.

These men have enriched the knowledge and enjoyment of people throughout the communities by giving archeological presentations at schools, civic organizations, historical societies and museums. Because of these showings, people of all ages not only learn about history, but they are able to see and hold the actual relics. Without the careful research done by Dan and Keith, we might never have known that the site of Robert Rogers' first battle on snowshoes could also be the scene of a later important battle in which the British army's beloved Lord Howe was killed.

Prelude

The French and Indian War, 1754-1763. These were years of magnificent battles and heroic men, fighting with chivalry and savageness in forts and forests.

This war gave rise to men of legend, like Montcalm and Wolfe, who faced each other on the Plains of Abraham in the Battle of Quebec. Montcalm, de Levis and Bourlamaque routed Abercromby's overwhelming force of 15,000 men at the log wall of Ticonderoga. Durantaye and Langy, with the French and Indians, utterly defeated Robert Rogers and his Rangers in the cold, snow covered, thickly forested hills of the Trout Brook Valley in the epic Battle on Snowshoes.

And who does not thrill to read of the gallant defense of forts such as William Henry in 1757 by Colonel Monro, or the superb defense of Niagara by Captain Pouchot and his exhausted French force in 1758?

All of these battles and their locations are documented and well known. But there are still some battles whose locations, mysteriously enough, have never been found. Two of these are the First Battle on Snowshoes (also known as the Battle of La Barbue Creek, or the Smaller Snowshoe Battle) and the location of the ambush and death of Lord Howe following the landing of Abercromby's army in July of 1758. Documentation and evidence exists to point the way, but the actual battlesites have never been confirmed.

Until now.

PART ONE

The Battles

Rangers prepare to ambush French sleighs

1757

Ambush In The Snow

Captain Robert Rogers ghosted through the dripping cedar trees to a vantage point on the shore of Lake Champlain. The mist was profound; it shrouded the surrounding hills, blanketing them with gloom almost down to the snow covered shoreline.

As he crouched there, eyes scanning the frozen lake, he heard the rustle of his detachment coming up behind him. The sounds were as familiar as his own breathing: the shuffling of the snowshoes, the creaking of wet leather straps and cartridge boxes, and the occasional rattle of a powder horn or a tomahawk against the musket each man carried close to his body.

This scout, which was his biggest to date,[1] had started three days earlier from Fort Edward on January 15, 1757. Rogers and his 49 Rangers were accompanied by Ens. Caleb Page and Lt. John Stark, his close friend and most able officer. When they arrived at Fort William Henry on Lake George, the commander, Major Eyre, granted Rogers an additional 33 men led by Capt. Thomas Speakman, who would be second in command. Other officers among those 33 men included Lt. Samuel Kennedy, Ensign Brewer and Ens. James Rogers, the older brother of Robert.

The force of 85 men left the safety of the stout log walls of Fort William Henry in the late afternoon of January 17.[2] The snow on the ground was three to four feet deep, so they proceeded down Lake George on the ice and camped that night near the first narrows. In the morning, after carefully scrutinizing his Rangers, Rogers ordered back 11 men who were unable to keep up, either from frostbite or from having fallen on the ice.[3] The remaining force of 74, officers and enlisted men included, continued north and camped on the west side of Lake George that evening.[4] On the next evening they made camp in the drizzling rain approximately three miles west of Lake Champlain, somewhere between the French forts of Carillon (called Ticonderoga by the English) and St. Frederic[5] (called Crown Point by the English). Here, amid the massive trunks of gray, naked beeches and dark brown hemlocks, the Rangers dug their fire pits down through the softened snow to ground level and attempted to dry out their wet muskets and sodden clothes.

Early the next morning they ate their rations and began to move east toward Lake Champlain, keeping to the high ground along the ravines that followed Fivemile Creek to its entrance in the lake. That entrance marked a point approximately five miles between both forts. It was here that Robert Rogers' keen eyes spotted movement down the lake. Two sleighs were headed up from Carillon to St. Frederic.

Immediately Rogers ordered John Stark and 20 of his men north to stop the sleighs as they came abreast of Capt. Speakman and his party, who would anchor the main ambush point.[6] Rogers and his group would dash in behind and cut off the expected attempt to escape back to the safety of Carillon.

Rogers watched his men disperse as the sleighs drew nearer. Moments later, much to his surprise, he spied ten additional sleighs following the others at a distance. Hoping to bag the bigger prize by letting the first two sleighs pass, Rogers dispatched two swift messengers to tell Stark of the new plan,[7] but the lead sleighs reached the killing ground first, and John Stark led his Rangers onto the ice. Seeing their

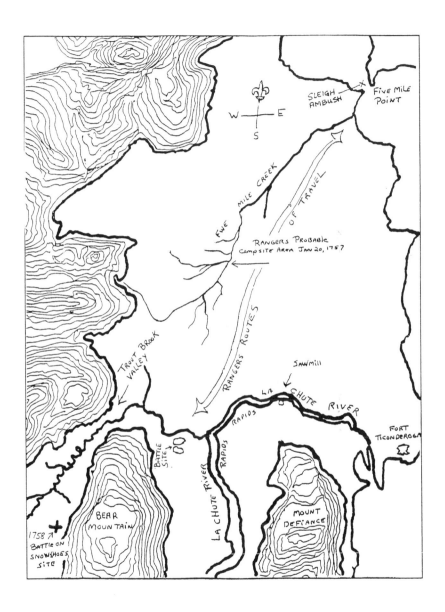

Map showing area of 1757 ambushes. (Map A)

trap sprung too early, Rogers, Speakman and the rest of the Ranger force leapt from their concealment and captured three sleighs and seven French prisoners.[8] The drivers of the other sleighs wheeled around in frantic haste and headed back to Carillon to alert Commandant Lusignan and the garrison.

Upon interrogation, the seven prisoners painted an ominous picture for Rogers and his men. Besides the normal garrison of 350 men at Carillon, there had recently arrived a group of approximately 250 Canadians and Indians.[9] Hundreds of French troops also manned St. Frederic, where additional raiding parties were expected soon.

Robert Rogers was now between the proverbial rock and hard place. He knew the garrison at the fort to his rear immediately would be alerted to this morning's ambush, and they probably would send out a force to try to locate him. They would easily find his detachment's snow-packed trail to the site of the ambush. Rogers' wisest choice would be to return to Fort William Henry by observing the common Ranger rule of taking a different route. But this would mean crossing the lake and possibly being seen by scouts from the French forts, or going back by a new way parallel to the way they had come. Either of these choices meant breaking a new trail through the soft, wet snow; fatiguing and time-consuming to say the least. Or he could return as quickly as possible by his original route.

In the collaborative statement made by Ranger Privates Shutes and Eastman, "after taking the sleds a council of war advised to return by a different route from that by which the party came, which was the usual practice of the Rangers, and on this occasion would have enabled them to escape the hazards of a battle. Rogers, however, said in regard to the enemy, that they would dare not pursue him, and took the same route back."[10]

Let us put ourselves in Rogers' shoes, in order to understand why he made this decision. His men have snowshoed north through waist-deep snow and have a packed-down trail on which to return. This path is the quickest, easiest and least fatiguing route home. He hopes, with any kind of luck, that he can get back past the anticipated blocking force before they can find and meet him.

He also thinks this: since the beginning of his legendary scouting, he has never been defeated. He is 24 years old and at the peak of his strength and cockiness. If he can't beat the French in his footrace to safety, then he will kick the hell out of anyone who gets in his way. He orders his men with "all possible expedition" to return to the previous night's bivouac and rekindle the fires in order to dry their guns, which by this time have been exposed to the damp weather for several hours.[11]

This decision was, in retrospect, the wisest decision that Rogers made during the course of that day's events. For it meant that the messy sludge of wet, fouled black powder had been removed from the men's guns; barrels and locks were dried, and charges of fresh, dry powder were rammed home. Being hunters and woodsmen, some of the Rangers also might have covered their musket locks with a greased leather cover, and perhaps placed a wooden plug or tompion in the barrel for extra protection in keeping the powder dry.

Meanwhile, at 9:00 that same morning at Carillon, an officer of the French colony troops by the name of DeRouilly received orders from the commandant to proceed with sleighs to Fort St. Frederic and return with supplies and forage. He was to be escorted by 15 soldiers and one sergeant.[12] By the time all the men were assembled and the horses were harnessed, in the traces and on their way, it was past 9:30. Two of the sleighs made rapid time and pulled far ahead. Shortly thereafter, the remaining ten sleighs picked their way through the softened snow and trampled through the mud on the packed trail that led to the ice of Lake Champlain. Here they made better time as they headed north to St. Frederic. Luckily for them, their comrades led by a considerable distance, and what had begun as another boring soldiers' detail suddenly became a frantic dash for survival when the English Rangers charged out of ambush at Fivemile Point.

At approximately 11:30 a.m., Paul Louis Lusignan, captain and commandant of the garrison at Carillon, was busy in his officer's room when he heard the shouts and clamor of men outside on the parade ground.[13] Opening the door, he saw through the misty rain a steaming, panting horse covered with mud and snow, obviously ridden hard. Its rider was already bounding toward him, flushed with excitement.

Quickly and breathlessly, the courier recounted the startling events to Lusignan. There had been an ambush of the sleigh detail, about halfway to Fort St. Frederic, by about 100 English Rangers. Close behind the courier came the rest of the sleighs, led by DeRouilly, who corroborated the soldier's account.

Captain Lusignan promptly ordered his officers to assemble and meet in his quarters. In that crowded room, hurried choices and decisions were made. Since the Rangers had attacked the convoy from the western shore, it stood to reason that their route of travel had been north and west of Carillon, probably following the *Route des Agniers*, or Mohawk Trail, through the mountain valley west of the French posts. The Rangers could have crossed the lake and returned down the east side of it after the ambush, but that was thought unlikely. If they did, it would be almost impossible to plot their course and set an ambush.

However, if they were foolish enough to return upon their same outgoing trail, perhaps it could be found in time to catch them in an ambush. It was Lusignan's best—and, probably—his only choice.

Studying the room carefully, his eyes quickly fell upon the kind of leader equal to the woodsmanship of the English Rangers: Ens. Charles-Michel Mouet de Langlade of *Les Compagnies Franches de la Marine,* who had arrived in December at the head of approximately 90 Chippewa and

Ottawa warriors. Langlade was already the stuff legends were made of in *la petite guerre*, the savage, no-holds-barred war of the forests.

Five years earlier, Langlade, along with the Ottawa war chief Pontiac, had led an expedition to destroy the frontier post and village of Pickawillany, in present-day Ohio. The people of this village, then in the heart of French-claimed territory, had openly sided with the English and their traders, in defiance of the French. They were led by a chief named Unemakemi, also called "Old Britain" or "La Demoiselle."

In June of 1752 the force of over 250 warriors led by Langlade and Pontiac struck Pickawillany without warning. The annihilation was complete; the post was burned and the village destroyed. "La Demoiselle" was killed, as were many of his followers. His heart was then cut out and boiled along with the bodies of some of the English traders.[14] To the horrified survivors the message was clear: the English had been overthrown. The tribes must align themselves with the French. There could be no other way.

Later, in 1755, Langlade was credited with helping to lay the ambush that destroyed the massive British army under Gen. Edward Braddock near the banks of the Monongahela not far from Ft. Duquesne.[15] Charles Langlade was one of the fiercest partisan fighters of the French and Indian War.

Langlade and his Indians were well used to the tactics of *la petite guerre*. Equipped with snowshoes (*raquettes*), they were sent out immediately to find the trail of the Rangers and to pick a suitable ambush spot if possible.[16]

In the meantime the call to action was sounded, and the French troops were assembled on the fort parade ground. A force of almost 90 men was selected from the regiments of La Reine, Languedoc, Roussillon, and Les Compagnies Franches to follow Langlade's Canadians and Indians.

Officer, Les Compagnies Franches de la Marine

The detachment marched out of the fort at approximately 12:30 and was under the command of Captain De Basserode and Lieutenant D'Astral of Languedoc, and Captain Granville of the Regiment La Reine. The French regular troops were not equipped or familiar with snowshoes.[17]

Slowly and inexorably, the two opposing forces headed toward the place where their paths would meet; and the tomb-like silence of the northern woods would be shattered by the roaring of muskets and the shouts and cries of combatants bent on destroying each other.

In the meantime, by about 1 or 1:30 p.m. Rogers' men had sufficiently dried their muskets. (See Chapter 3 for a detailed description of this process.) They ate a hurried meal and pushed on toward Fort William Henry. Rogers gave orders to his men who were guarding the French prisoners to kill them immediately if attacked, to prevent the prisoners from giving information as to the true size of the Ranger force.[18]

Along with Lieutenant Kennedy, Rogers led the way southward with Captain Speakman in the center and John Stark bringing up the rear of the detachment. They advanced a mile and a half over broken ground.[19] Just as the front of the column had passed a valley of fifteen rods breadth and gained the summit of a western hill,[20] the woods exploded in a flash of fire and smoke; and the Rangers came face to face with Charles-Michel de Langlade and the French force waiting in ambush. Robert Rogers had lost the gambled foot-race. Now only a miracle could save him from losing his men's lives and the battle which was now upon him in full fury.

The miracle that Rogers so desperately needed came in two unforeseen forms. Although the French force had arrived at the ambush site first, it was not by much. The force of French regulars was met and guided to the ambush site by scouts from Langlade's party. As they left the hard snow-packed road that went to the sawmill and beyond, they struggled through the now knee-deep snow with great difficulty, most having only shoes or moccasins on their feet. Their progress was exhausting and maddeningly slow. Finally the regulars came to the spot Langlade had selected, having found the Rangers' tracks and then proceeded north to his chosen killing ground. There the French troops deployed in a semi-circle on the top of a hill along the Rangers' southward return route, and settled down to wait in the cold, drizzly rain. Unknown to them, this helped cause the first miracle that Rogers needed to escape annihilation. Since being drawn up on the parade ground, the French soldiers' muskets had been exposed to the steady, light rain. By now it was about 2:30 p.m. All through the long march to the battlesite, and now as the men sat and waited, the hydroscopic properties of black powder were rendering many of the firearms useless. When Rogers, Kennedy and the vanguard topped the rise of ground and the French order to fire was given, only about half of the French fusils went off.

Rogers, whose personal luck was always good in battle, sustained a grazing wound to the forehead, knocking him down but not out. Others were not so lucky. Lieutenant Kennedy and a man named Gardiner were killed outright, along with several others. Rogers and his men turned and ran back down the valley as quickly as possible. The French, exasperated by the deplorable misfiring of their weapons, bolted out of cover and, raising hue and cry, plunged through the snow to attack with fixed bayonets. Some of the wounded and slower Rangers met their demise at the point of cold steel.[21]

The second part of Robert Rogers' much-needed miracle now manifested itself in the human form of Lt. John Stark, who, with an eye to detail and quick mind to seize the opportunity, had deployed the rest of the Ranger force in a rear guard covering position on the opposite hill, the higher of the two. This bold, quick maneuver provided a covering fire for Rogers and his fleeing Rangers, and also gave them the high, choice ground.

The concentrated Ranger fire from the top of the hill drove the French back down the slope and to cover. A few half-hearted attempts were made to flank the Rangers' strong position, but without their *raquettes* the French attempts were futile. Finally, as the afternoon wore on, both sides settled down to long-range sniping at each other.

It was during this sniping action that John Stark made the only fatal shot in his long military career that he could later recall. While firing from his position atop the hill, Stark noticed that several balls struck close by him, coming from a certain direction. Moments later he noticed an Indian stretched full length upon a boulder behind a tree. Stark fired and shot the Indian through the head, and the Indian rolled off the boulder into the snow, which Stark stated was "four feet deep on the level ground."[22]

Another boulder figured prominently in the battle account of Ranger Private Thomas Brown. Although there are some inaccuracies in Brown's report (date, number of sleighs), his general observations are well worth reading. I have taken the opportunity to include a portion of Brown's "Narrative" printed in Boston, 1760, by Draper and Fowle:

"On the 18th of Jan. 1757, we marched on a scout from Fort William Henry; Major Rogers himself headed us. All were voluntiers that went on this scout. We came to the road leading from Tionderoga to Crown Point, and on Lake Champlain (which was froze over) we saw about 50 sleys; the Major thought proper to attack them and ordered us all, about 60 in number, to lay in ambush, and when they were near enough we were ordered to pursue them. I happened to be near the Major when he took the first prisoner, a Frenchman. I singled out one and followed him. They fled some one way and some another, but soon I came up with him and took him. We took seven in all, the rest escaping, some to Crown Point and

some returned to Tionderoga. When we had brought the prisoners to land, the Major examined them, and they inform'd him that there were 35 Indians and 500 regulars at Tionderoga. It being a rainy day we made a fire and dry'd our guns. The Major tho't best to return to Fort William Henry in the same path we came, the snow being very deep; we march'd in an Indian file and kept the Prisoners in the rear, lest we should be attack'd. We proceeded in this order about a mile and a half, and as we were ascending a Hill, and the Centre of our men were at the top, the French, to the number of 400 besides 30 or 40 Indians, fired on us before we discovered them. The Major ordered us to advance. I receiv'd a wound from the enemy (the first shot they made on us) thro' the body, upon which I retir'd into the rear, to the prisoner I had taken on the lake, knock'd him on the head and killed him, lest he should escape and give information to the enemy; and as I was going to place myself behind a large rock, there started up an Indian from the other side; I threw myself backward into the snow and it being very deep, sunk so low that I broke my snowshoes (I had time to pull 'em off, but was obliged to let my shoes go with them). One Indian threw his Tomahawk at me, and another was just upon seizing me; but I happily escaped and got to the centre of our men, and fix'd myself behind a large Pine, where I loaded and fired every opportunity; after I had discharged 6 or 7 times, there came a ball and cut off my gun just at the lock. About half an hour after I receiv'd a shot in my knee; I crawled again into the rear, and as I was turning about receiv'd a shot in my shoulder. The engagement held, as near as I could guess 5 ½ hours, and as I learnt after I was taken, we killed more of the enemy than we were in number. By this time it grew dark and the firing ceased on both sides, and as we were so few the Major took the advantage of the night and escaped with his well men, without informing the wounded of his design, lest they should inform the enemy and they should pursue him before he had got out of their reach.

Capt. Spikeman, one Robert Baker and myself, all very badly wounded, made a small fire and sat about half an hour, when looking around we could not see any of our men; Captain Spikeman called to Major Rogers, but received no answer, except from the enemy at some distance; upon this we concluded that our people were fled. All hope of escape now vanish'd; we were so wounded that we could not travel; I could but just walk, the others could scarce move; we therefore concluded to surrender ourselves to the French; Just as we came to this conclusion, I saw an Indian coming towards us over a small rivulet that parted us in the engagement: I crawl'd so far from the fire that I could not be seen, though I could see what was acted at the fire; the Indian came to Capt.

*Spikeman, who was not able to resist, and stripp'd and scalp'd him alive;
Baker, who was lying by the Captain, pull'd out his knife to stab himself,
which the Indian prevented and carried him away. Seeing this dreadful
tragedy, I concluded, if possible, to crawl into the woods and there die of
my wounds: but not being far from Capt. Spikeman, he saw me and beg'd
me for God's sake! To give him a Tomahawk, that he might put an end to
his life! I refus'd him, and exhorted him as well as I could to pray for
mercy, as he could not live many minutes in that deplorable condition,
being on the frozen ground, cover'd with snow. He desir'd me to let his
Wife know (if I lived to get home) the dreadful death he died. As I was
travelling as well as I could, or rather creeping along, I found one of our
people dead; I pull'd off his Stockings (he had no shoes) and put them on
my own legs.*

*By this time the enemy had made a fire, and had a large number of
Centries out on our path, so that I was obliged to creep quite around them
before I could get into the path; but just before I came to it I saw a
Frenchman behind a tree, within two rods of me, but the fire shining right
on him prevented his seeing me. They cried out about every Quarter of an
hour in French, All is Well! And while he that was so near me was
speaking, I took the opportunity to creep away, that he might not hear me,
and by this manner got clear of him and got into our path. But the snow
and cold put my feet into such pain, as I had no shoes, that I could not go
on; I therefore sat down by a brook, and wrapt my feet in my blanket. But
my body being cold by sitting still, I got up, and crawl'd along in the
miserable condition the remainder of the night.*

*The next day, about 11 o'clock, I heard the shouts of Indians behind
me, and I suppos'd they saw me; within a few minutes four came down a
mountain, running towards me: I threw off my blanket, and fear and
dread quickened my pace for a while; but by reason of the loss of so much
blood from my wounds, I soon failed. When they were within a few rods of
me they cock'd their guns, and told me to stop but I refus'd, hoping that
they would fire and kill me on the spot; which I chose, rather than the
dreadful death Capt. Spikeman died of. They soon came up with me, took
me by the neck and kiss'd me. On searching my pockets they found some
money, which they were so fond of, that in trying who could get most,
they had like to have killed me. They took some dry leaves and put them
into my wounds, and then turn'd about and ordered me to follow them.*

*When we came near the main body of the enemy, the Indians made a
live-shout, as they call it when they bring in a prisoner alive (Different
from the shout they make when they bring in scalps, which they call a
dead shout.) The Indians ran to meet us, and one of them struck me with a*

cutlass across the side; he cut thro my cloaths, but did not touch my flesh; others ran against me with their heads: I ask'd if there was no interpreter, upon which a Frenchman cry'd, I am one: I ask'd him, if this was the way they treated their prisoners, to let them be cut to pieces by the Indians? He desired me to come to him; but the Indians would not let me, holding me one by one arm and one by the other: But there arising a difference between the four Indians that took me, they fell to fighting, which their commanding Officer seeing, he came and took me away and carry'd me to the interpreter; who drew his sword, and pointing it to my breast, charged me to tell the truth, or he would run me through: He then ask'd me what number our scout consisted of? I told him 50: He asked where they were going? I told him, I supposed as they were so numerous they could best tell. He said I told him wrong; for he knew of more than 100 that were slain; I told him we had lost but 19 in all. He said, there were as many officers. On which he led me to Lieut. Kennedy. I saw he was much Tomahawk'd by the Indians. He asked me if he was an Officer: I told him he was a Lieutenant: and then he took me to another; who I told him, was an Ensign (Caleb Page); thence he carried me to Captain Spikeman, who was lying in the place I left him; they had cut off his head, and fix'd it on a pole.

I beg'd for a pair of shoes, and something to eat; the interpreter told me, I should have relief when I came to Tionderoga, which was but one mile and ¼ off, and then delivered me to the four Indians that took me. The Indians gave me a piece of bread, and put a pair of shoes on my feet."[23]

Using darkness as their cover, Rogers and his remaining Rangers had slipped stealthily around the French, who were between them and safety. Upon reaching Lake George, Rogers dispatched Lieutenant Stark, Private Thomas Burnside and another Ranger private to proceed with all haste to Fort William Henry and procure sleighs for the wounded. Stark and the others reached the fort exhausted, but safe; and a relief party of 15 Rangers, commanded by Lieutenant Bulkeley of Hobbs' Company, met Rogers and his tired remnants at the first narrows of Lake George.

As Thomas Brown limped to Carillon escorted by his tawny captors, the gloomy, overcast sky faded into darkness. Soon the snow started to fall, as it would do many more times throughout the winter. The bodies of the dead, the broken muskets, dropped and spent bullets, shoes, coins and accoutrements, all lay buried under the white blanket of snow.

In the spring the snow melted into slush, then water, then mud. The remains from the battle settled into the Adirondack soil. Soon the rays of the sun would bring forth ferns, grasses and sedges; and these in turn would further help hide the fallen soldiers and their equipment. Finally, the splendid hues of the Adirondack fall—the red sumacs, the brilliant scarlet of the sugar maples, the bright yellow beeches and somber brown of the oaks, mixed with mauve and gold and pierced by the green spires of the pines, hemlocks, and spruces—all these leaves would fall one by one to cover the remnants with the blanket of autumn.

Two hundred and forty years of winters, springs, summers and falls have passed and helped to cover and hide these relics, the site of Rogers' first major battle in the snow. For 240 years the exact location of battlesite has remained a mystery, and the relics have been forgotten and lost.

Until now.

Ambush in the Snow

Sources

1. Steele, p. 74
2. Roby, p. 28
3. Roby, p. 28; Loescher, *History*, p. 118
4. Roby, p. 28
5. Ibid.
6. Ibid.
7. Loescher, *History*, p. 121; Cuneo, p. 46
8. Roby, p. 28
9. Roby, p. 29
10. Loescher, *History*, p. 340
11. Roby, p. 29
12. Loescher, *History*, pp. 346-347
13. Bougainville, p. 81
14. Slocum, pp. 99-100
15. Kopperman, pp. 26, 282, 283; *Dictionary of Canadian Biography*, Vol. IV, pp. 563-564
16. Bougainville, p. 81
17. Ibid.
18. Loescher, *History*, p. 236
19. Loescher, *History*, p. 332
20. Roby, p. 29
21. Loescher, *History*, p. 346, Bougainville, p. 81
22. Stark, p. 19
23. Loescher, *History*, p. 334

British Officer

1758

The Bridge, the Brigadier and the Hill

The day is hot and humid as I stand here on the hill, as it probably was 241 years ago, in July 1758. Insects still drone, and the heady scent of pine wafts down the hill on a stray breeze.

A lot has changed, however, in 241 years. Where there were virgin forests of huge pines and oaks that covered the hillside, and indeed even the mountain, there now is a new growth of smaller hardwood trees, interspersed with evergreens. Near the bottom of the hill is an overgrown meadow that falls away into a swampy marshland near the brook. The Indian paths and French patrol trails are now streets and highways like Route 9N, over which travel cars, trucks and vans in a seemingly never-ending caravan to and from the village of Ticonderoga. To the north and east of the hill stand the houses, stores and buildings of the town; to the west a motel, lumber yard and restaurant; to the south and east lie the beginnings of a trailer park.

But here where I stand is history, long gone unnoticed, undiscovered, and fortunately until now, undeveloped. When there are breaks in the noise of the traffic and hubbub of the village, especially in the magical hours of early dawn, one can still hear, if one listens closely, the gurgle of Trout

Brook as it flows eastward to join the more noisy, rushing and foamy waters of La Chute. The two waters merge together and cascade down through the village of Ticonderoga to the falls where the French had their sawmill. Here La Chute settles down to become the river that flows into Lake Champlain, still guarded by the black cannons of Fort Ticonderoga.

Two centuries ago, French soldiers destroyed a bridge which had carried them over those very waters. Two centuries ago, a brigadier charged up this hill to his destiny.

Following the debacles and defeats of the earlier years of the war, including Braddock's annihilation on the Mononga-hela in 1755, the fall of Forts Oswego and Bull in 1756, and the devastating loss of Fort William Henry in 1757, the pendulum finally began to swing the other way; and the fortunes of war would begin to favor the British. It began with the appointment of William Pitt to the post of England's Prime Minister. In 1758 William Pitt would be the powerful mastermind of British military operations, not only in America, but also in Europe, the Far East and on the high seas.

In 1758 the British planned to attack simultaneously the French fortress at Louisbourg on Cape Breton Island; Fort Duquesne, site of Braddock's defeat on the Monongahela; and Forts Carillon (Ticonderoga) and St. Frederic (Crown Point), sweeping up through the Champlain Valley to Montreal.[1]

To subdue the French on the Lake Champlain front, Pitt chose as his commander in chief, Major General James Abercromby, a Scot of 52 years of age. "Abercromby, raised to his place by political influence, was little but the nominal commander. 'A heavy man,' said British General James Wolfe in a letter to his father. 'An aged gentelman, infirm in body and mind,' wrote William Parkman, a boy of 17 who carried a musket in a Massachusetts regiment and kept in his knapsack a dingy little notebook in which he jotted down what passed each day."[2] William Parkman was the great-uncle of noted historian, Francis Parkman.

But Pitt was not without an ace up his sleeve. While the doddering Abercromby was the "nominal commander," he would be seconded in command by the bright, flashing sword of England: Lord George Augustus Viscount Howe, grandson of King George, special favorite of Pitt, and loved by both royalty and commoner, British and colonial, regular and provincial. The Brigadier.

General James Wolfe, who was later to achieve enduring fame in the siege and capture of Quebec in 1759, called Howe "The noblest Englishman that has appeared in my time, and the best soldier in the British Army." Pitt called him "a character of ancient times; a complete model of military virtue." He had the qualities of a leader of men. The entire army felt his presence, from general to drummer boy. He was its soul; and while breathing into it his own energy and ardor, and bracing it by stringent discipline, he broke through the traditions of the service and gave it new shapes to suit the time and place. During the previous year, he had studied the art of forest warfare and joined Rogers and his Rangers in their hardships, making himself one of them.[3] At 34 years of age, sound in mind and body, he was able and ready to lead His Majesty's forces in the proposed attacks on Forts Carillon and St. Frederic in the summer of 1758.

As the British readied their massive army, the French were in a quandary. Hearing countless rumors of proposed attacks, they had to find out where, when and how. Would these attacks come against Quebec or Louisbourg, or would they be against Forts Duquesne, Frontenac or Niagara? Or was it to be against Carillon and St. Frederic? Or could it possibly be all of them?

French scouts were sent forth to make raids, take prisoners and bring back information. Of all the partisan leaders, the one most trusted, the one most daring, and the one most reliable was "Montcalm's favorite scout,"[4] Ensign Jean Baptiste Levreault de Langis de Montegron, known as "Langis" to the French and "Langy" to the English. Robert Rogers referred to him as "Longee, the famous French Partisan."[5] Veteran of the sieges of Fort Beausejour, Fort Oswego, and the winter attack in 1757 and siege in August of that same year of Fort William Henry, master of the art of *la petite guerre*, leader of countless raids and ambushes, and the undisputed victor in the epic Battle on Snowshoes in March of 1758, where he nearly annihilated Robert Rogers and his Rangers, Langy was the one person the French could count on to find out the intentions of the English.

Louis Antoine de Bougainville, Montcalm's aide-de-camp, noted in his journals the following entries about Langy and his scouts in the weeks leading up to Abercromby's attack on Carillon: May 12-20—"M. de Langis has returned with three prisoners who have no information. He left again at once with all the Indians we have in this area to go and reconnoiter the major moves the enemy is reported to be making from Albany to Fort Edward." May 27—"M. de Langis has been in the field since the seventeenth with twenty five Indians." May 31—"Arrival of M. de Langis at Montreal. He took three scalps on the road from Albany to Fort Edward." June 13—"M. de Langis left for Carillon with eighty warriors."[6]

The British, in the meantime, tried to do what Montcalm had done the previous summer in his successful approach and siege of Fort William Henry—that is to say, throw out a protective screen of Rangers and scouts to shield the movements and build up of the main army from the French eyes. They were not as successful. On June 23 Rogers sent out four scouting parties of Rangers to cover the Lake George and South Bay regions. A party of 18 Rangers commanded by Lt. Simon Stevens was surrounded and captured on an island at the second narrows of Lake George by Langy and his men. They were then taken to Carillon for questioning by Col. Charles Francois de Bourlamaque, who had recently arrived and was commanding the troops there.[7] Learning of the impending English force, Bourlamaque dispatched Langy and his prisoners to warn Canadian Governor Vaudreuil of the dangerous situation. As he made his way north up Lake Champlain, Langy was met by the southward bound flotilla of French regiments, including the Marquis de Montcalm, Aide Bougainville and their staff. Relaying the information to Montcalm, Langy pressed on and reached Montreal on June 27. Here he passed on the prisoners and information to Vaudreuil and headed back to Carillon, eager to take part in the inevitable battle. He would not be disappointed.[8] After arriving back at Carillon, he was sent out once again. July 4: "This evening there departed, under the orders of Sieur de Langis, a detachment of about 150 men, 104 of them volunteers from our battalions, 25 Canadians, and a score of Indians. A fact worth noting and one which does us honor is that in this detachment, a captain and seven lieutenants of our regulars march under the orders of an Ensign; M. de Langis has only this rank. His orders are to go and observe the location, the number, and the movements of the enemy at the end of Lake St. Sacrement (Lake George) and to make prisoners if possible."[9]

Early in the morning of July 5, Abercromby's mighty armada sailed from the southern end of Lake George, where it had been encamped. Just imagine the scene as the grand attack was put into motion: over 900 bateaux, large numbers of flatboats carrying artillery, and 135 whaleboats completely covered the surface of the lake. The flotilla moved up toward the first narrows where Langy's force of 150 French and Indians in canoes watched the huge force come into sight. Langy turned his canoes northward and sped the news to Montcalm at Carillon.[10]

"Before ten in the morning, the British armada began its passage through the first narrows. From front to rear the line was six miles long. The spectacle was superb; the brightness of the summer day; the romantic beauty of the scenery; the sheen and sparkle of those crystal waters; the bordering mountains with their green summits and sunny crags; the flash of oars, and the notes of bugle, trumpet, bagpipe and drum, answered and prolonged by a hundred woodland echoes."[11] "I never beheld as delightful a prospect," wrote a wounded officer at Albany a fortnight later.[12]

This was reminiscent of Braddock's army crossing the Monongahela with trumpets blaring, drums pounding, colors unfurled in the breeze—a brave sight that young George Washington was to recall "the most thrilling of his life." The confidence of Abercromby's army was overwhelming. Here was a crusade to drive the French papist dogs out of Canada forever and to revenge the loss of Fort William Henry. This army viewed itself as unstoppable.

The flotilla moved forward until about five o'clock in the afternoon and halted at Sabbath Day Point for food and rest and to allow the slower artillery barges to catch up. It was here that Lord Howe, always inquisitive and probing, likely discussed with Ranger John Stark and others the best ways to approach Ticonderoga.[13]

At the same time, not many miles away at Carillon, Bougainville wrote in his journal: July 5—"...At five o'clock in the evening Sieur de Langy's detachment returned, having seen on the lake a great body of enemy barges which could only be what it was, the advance guard of their army, led by Colonel Bradstreet and Major Rogers. Orders given at once to the troops at the falls that at a general call by drum beat, they should spend the night in bivouac and should commence to clear away the camp equipment. The same order sent to the Portage to send out detachments to the north and south to observe the landing of the enemy. Consequently Sieur de Langy has been detached with 130 volunteers to take post between Mont Pélée and the lake; and Sieur de Trépezec, captain in the Bearn Regiment, supports him with three light companies."[14]

The English army began moving northward again at about 11 p.m. and entered the second narrows at daybreak. On its left was the landmark called Bald Mountain by the English and called Mont Pélée by the French. Today it is known as Rogers' Rock.

Lord Howe, with Rogers and Bradstreet and their picked troops, went in whaleboats to reconnoiter the landing. At the place which the French called the Contrecoeur (Burnt Camp), where Montcalm had embarked for the assault on Fort William Henry the summer before, they saw a detachment of the enemy too weak to oppose them. Their men landed and drove them off. At noon the whole army was on shore. Rogers, with a party of Rangers, was ordered forward to reconnoiter, and the troops were formed for the march.[15]

At this time a critical decision was made, one that would dictate a chain of disastrous events for the English. Bourlamaque, realizing the futility of trying to stop the overwhelming mass about to march against them, ordered his French troops to destroy the bridge at the head of the lake and fall back on the portage road to the sawmill. There they would also destroy the other and last bridge across La Chute.[16] Now the British were faced with a dilemma. Should they take the time and effort to try to rebuild the bridges and therefore have available to them the well-used portage road of the French, capable of transporting their artillery and

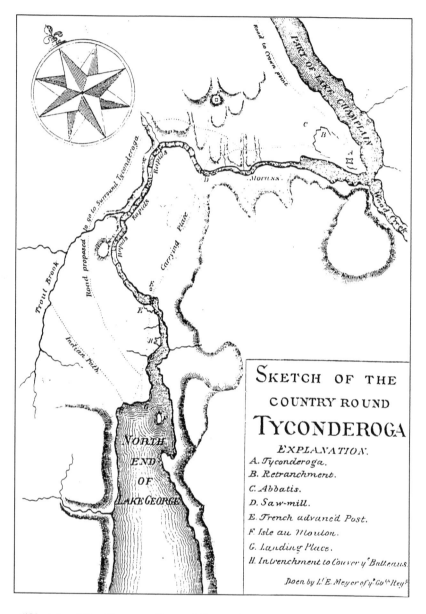

"Sketch of the Country Round Tyconderoga" by Lt. Elias Meyer of
ye 60th Regt., c. 1758. Lithograph by B. Meisel published in
Montcalm and Wolfe by Francis Parkman, Boston: Little, Brown,
1884. Collection of the Fort Ticonderoga Museum.

immense mountains of supplies and equipment? Or should they stay on the west side of the river and push on through the forest where they would eventually come out down at the sawmill and on the same side of the river where the portage road returned to lead to the fort?

Abercromby knew from his intelligence sources that Montcalm had less than 4,000 men to oppose the British force of 15,000. What he also knew, and didn't want to deal with, was the arrival of reinforcements that were supposed to be coming to the aid of Montcalm. Therefore, it was decided that time was of the essence and to push on with all haste alongside the river toward the sawmill. Brigadier General Lord Howe would lead the army. It was a fatal mistake.

From this part of the shore where the army had landed, the forest stretched northward half a mile or more to the mountains, behind which lay the valley of Trout Brook. On this low ground the army began its march in four columns with the intention of passing around the western bank of the river. Rogers, with the provincial regiments of Fitch and Lyman, led the way at some distance before the rest. The forest was extremely dense and heavy and the ground was encumbered with fallen trees in every stage of decay. It was so obstructed with undergrowth that it was impossible to see more than a few yards in any direction.

"The ranks were broken, and the men struggled on as best they could in dampness and shade under a canopy of boughs that the sun could scarcely pierce. The difficulty increased when after advancing about a mile, they came upon undulating and broken ground. They were not far from the upper rapids of the outlet. The guides became bewildered in the maze of trunks and boughs; the marching columns were confused and fell in one upon the other. They were in the strange situation of an army lost in the woods."[17]

A· LANDED ON THE 6ᵀᴴ OF JULY AND MARCHED IN FOUR COLUMNS,
THREE FRENCH BATTALIONS RETIRING WITH GREAT PRECIPITATION
OVER THE FIRST BRIDGE AND BREAKING IT DOWN. COLUMNS SOON
IN GREAT DISORDER FROM THE THICKNESS OF THE WOOD. B· FELL
IN WITH THE FRENCH PICQUETS C·PART OF THE ARMY LAY THAT
NIGHT IN THE WOODS. THE REMAINDER LOST THEMSELVES AND
RETURNED TO THE LANDING PLACE: ON THE 7ᵀᴴ OF JULY, THE SOLDIERS
HAVING LOST THEIR PROVISIONS, THE WHOLE TROOPS RETURNED TO ·
THE LANDING PLACE, THAT EVENING THE WHOLE ARMY CROSSED
THE TWO BRIDGES, LAY ON THEIR ARMS THAT NIGHT, AND
ATTACKED THE ENEMY'S ENTRENCHMENT EARLY NEXT
MORNING ON THE 8ᵀᴴ OF JULY.

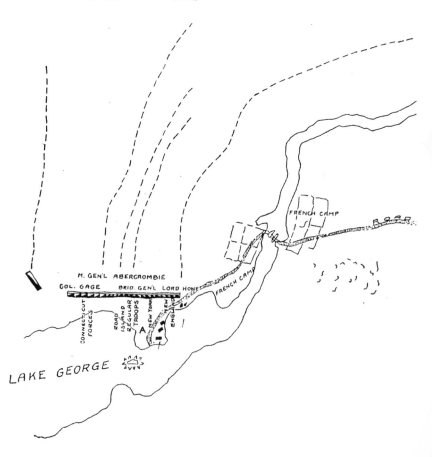

"Copy of a Map in the Possession of the Marquis of Sligo Sent Home by Captain Monypenny with the Report of Lord Howe's Death" Collection of the Fort Ticonderoga Museum.

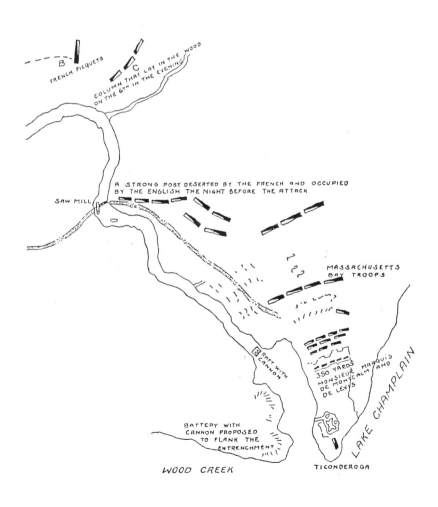

At about three o'clock, the detachment led by Langy and Trépezec was finally off the mountain coming down the last hill. Ahead was the Bernetz River (Trout Brook) and to the east the foamy, roaring waters of La Chute. With any luck the force would be back at Carillon in less than two hours.

Now the hand of fate, which no one can control, played another card. The 350-man force under Langy and Trépezec, who was under orders to "proceed as far as Mont Pélée and resist with all his might any troops who might come across country, as we supposed they would,"[18] found itself in a peculiar dilemma. The English army, they observed, had already landed and was probably readying itself for an assault across the portage bridge. They were not in any position to stop the English or help in the defense of the bridge if needed. They might have known that the bridge was destroyed, or perhaps not. They might have been able to see the English moving alongside the river from their lofty perch upon Mont Pélée and the adjoining hills, or perhaps not. And if they could have seen and shadowed the movement of the English, perhaps they might have planned an ambush, or perhaps not. At any rate it was decided to start heading back to Carillon. But Bougainville said, "However the 350 man detachment, which Sieur de Langy led, abandoned by the few Indians who served it as guides, went astray in the mountains and after twelve hours marching came into contact with an English column which was proceeding toward the Bernetz River."[19]

Suddenly everything seemed to go wrong. As the lead members of the French were almost to the bottom of the hill, they noticed other men, lots of them, coming along parallel to their own course. Puzzled, one of the French challenged, *"Qui vive?"* The other column stopped and stared back, guns at the ready. A voice cried back, *"Francais!"* but both sides knew better. Muskets fired and roared like thunder, lighting up the gloomy forest with fiery flashes of red; and clouds of white smoke hung in the humid forest obscuring the vision.

The French, coming in between companies of English and American troops, not knowing they were about to be encircled, dug in, hid behind trees and boulders, and started to make a fight of it.

Suddenly, up the forested hill charged an officer, resplendent in scarlet with shining buttons and white lace, yelling to his men, rugged and rash in the strength of his youth—a leader men would rally to and follow; a leader whose appearance would catch the keen eyes of the enemy, and whose breast would draw the sights of French fusils like a magnet.

The man was close; the charge was ready; and the flint was sharp. With a strong, steady pressure on the trigger and the front sight centered on the officer's chest, the fusil fired without hesitation; and the .60 caliber lead ball smashed into its target, taking the officer completely off his feet and throwing him backwards. As he hit the duff of the forest floor with a thud, men frantically raced toward him; but it was too late. The Brigadier was dead.

Cuneo found this eye witness account: "When the firing began on part of the Left Column, Lord Howe thinking it would be of the greatest Consequence, to beat the Enemy with the Light Troops, so as not to stop the march of the Main Body, went up with them, and had just gained the Top of the Hill, where the fighting was, when he was killed. Never Ball had a more Deadly Direction...I was about six yards from him, ...he fell on his Back and never moved, only his Hands quivered an instant."[20]

Another source says, "At the first volley they fired, they killed Lord Howe and Lieutenant Cumberfort. Lord Howe was at the head of the Rangers, notwithstanding all the remonstrances made him; the moment the fire was received in front, panic seized our soldiers; entire regiments flung themselves one atop of the other, and even the General narrowly escaped being dragged off in the confusion by the fugitives."[21]

Parkman says, "All was confusion. The dull, vicious reports of musketry in thick woods, at first few and scattering, then in fierce and rapid volleys, reached the troops behind. They could hear, but see nothing. Already harassed and perplexed, they became perturbed. For all they knew, Montcalm's whole army was upon them."[22]

Who fired that fatal shot? No one will ever know. I personally have always thought that it might have been Langy or one of his Canadian scouts. We know that both Langy and Trépezec, being leaders, were most likely to be near the front of the column. Both were part of the 50 French who managed to cross the river to safety before their force was completely surrounded. Both were wounded—Langy received a leg wound while crossing the river and Trépezec later died of his wound after being brought to the fort.[23]

An extract from a letter from Albany dated July 10, 1758, reads, "Our army, consisting of 16,000 men, set off from Fort William Henry the 5th Inst. And landed at the narrows the 6th in the morning without any opposition; a large division with Lord Howe at their head moved towards the Fort but were met within about two miles of Ticonderoga, at the sawmill by a large body of the enemy, on which a hot engagement ensued: at the beginning Lord Howe was shot dead, it is said by a French Officer, who it is said Capt. Henry Piney immediately shot; his Lordship is universally lamented by both the army and all others."[24]

Pouchot stated, "Lord Ho (Howe) was killed in this skirmish. His death was an irreparable loss for the enemy since he alone knew the terrain."[25]

"The fall of this noble and brave officer," said Rogers, "seemed to produce an almost general languor and consternation through the whole army."

"In Lord Howe," wrote another contemporary, Major Thomas Mante, "the soul of General Abercromby's army seemed to expire. From the unhappy moment the General was deprived of his advice, neither order nor discipline was observed, and a strange kind of infatuation usurped the place of resolution." The death of one man was the ruin of fifteen thousand.[26]

Finally, Bougainville summed up the loss in the eyes of the French. "His death stopped the advance. The disheartened English gave us twenty-four hours delay, and this precious time was the saving of us and of the colony."[27]

The delay had indeed given Montcalm and his French troops the time that they needed. Rutledge says it best: "Montcalm fully recognized the importance of this post and exerted every effort to see that it was properly defended. This was the best he could do. Vaudreuil would not provide the men and Bigot would not assure the necessary supplies except at exorbitant cost. But beyond that was the fact, patent to a soldier of Montcalm's experience, that, placed as he was, any general, good or bad, was bound to attempt to cut him off from his base. Ticonderoga, stretching out into the lake, made it next to impossible for an enterprising man to fail. Montcalm saw it all too clearly. Instead of attempting the impossible, he moved his force backward to a ridge about half a mile west of the fort. On it he built a rough embankment made of trunks of trees piled on one another to a height of nine feet. In front the trees had been leveled for perhaps five hundred feet. They lay where they had fallen, their tangled of branches leaning forward, sharpened and dreadful. On either side the land fell away in bottomless marshy ground that was almost as effective. As a fortification it didn't look impressive. It remained to be proven whether behind even so formidable a barrier three and a half thousand men could possibly make head against fifteen thousand."[28]

Without Howe's advice and counsel, Abercromby decided on a frontal assault without artillery—a *coup de musketrie*—to carry the day for him. That fateful day, July 8, was one of the bloodiest defeats in England's history with almost 2,000 casualties. The Black Watch Highland Regiment alone suffered 647 casualties, which was over half of its strength.[29] The troops of Montcalm, outnumbered five to one, had defeated the great army of Abercromby and sent it back down the lake in fear and disgrace.

Which brings us to a point of controversy that remains yet today: Amidst all this confusion, what happened to Lord Howe's body? The scene is one of panic and chaos; Howe's troops have just been surprised by the ambush and shocked by his sudden death; the grand army was stunned by defeat and Abercromby surely was numb with disbelief as he withdrew down the lake. Orders were given to transport the corpse to Albany. Supposedly, the Brigadier was buried there at St. Peter's Episcopal Church, where today one can see two plaques dedicated to his memory. But there are no records of the burial, nor are there any existing newspaper notices announcing a funeral for this famous man. In 1889, a laborer digging near the village of Ticonderoga unearthed a body with a stone inscribed, "Mem of Lo Howe killed Trout Brook." Many people think the "Lord Howe Stone" was a hoax, but neither burial place has ever been proven beyond doubt. While every attempt *should* have been made to retrieve the Brigadier's body and give him a proper burial, what do you think really happened on that stifling July day after a debilitating battle?

Things have changed in 241 years. The bridge that the French destroyed, that stopped the advance of the English and made them follow the river is now gone, replaced by another at a different location. The Brigadier, brilliant in scarlet, eager for battle, who led his men in the charge up the hill, is dead, buried only who knows where. But the hill is still here with the mountain behind it standing silent witness to the tragic, savage battle that occurred on its slopes.

It is early morning, June 25, 1999. I have come down from Mont Pélée with my wife Holly, my son Cliff, his wife Terri, and our good friend Greg Geiger. We have spent the night on the mountain in memory of Langy's and Trépezec's forces. I've been camping here for quite a few years now. We stand on the spot where it all happened so long ago. In a while we will head to Fort Ticonderoga and participate in the "Grande Encampment." But for now we are just content to pause and let our thoughts take us back to that fateful day when the young Brigadier lost his life on this hill.

Two hundred forty years of winters, springs, summers and falls have passed and helped to cover and hide the relics and remains of this battle. For 240 years the exact location of the battlesite has remained a mystery, and the relics have been forgotten and lost.

Until now.

CENTENNIAL POEM
by Hon. Clayton H. Delano, 1864

VI.

Just by the brook near yon eventful shade
Where foaming water forms a wild cascade
Where Ive's clustering tendrills twine
Round the gnarled oak and scraggy stunted pine

Here, once a forest waved, by that run
Gleamed glistening bayonets in the noon-day sun.
Here foe met foe; here flashed the burnished steel
As rank on rank now charge or backward reel.
While crackling rifles drowned the noisy flood
And robed the scene in anguish and in blood.
The Britons conquered, yet no cheer was heard
The deepest feeling every bosom stirred.
That night they slept, not on the victors' bed
They could not sleep -- the gallant Howe was dead.

TICONDEROGA
by Percy MacKay, 1909

QUI VIVE? Their muskets flare the wood;
  FRANCAIS! Their wild cheers start;
Lord Howe is dropt down where he stood,
  A hot ball through his heart.
They drive them back, they drown their boast
  In blood and the rushing river,
But the heart of Abercromby's host -
  The Lord of Hosts deliver!

★ ★ ★ ★ ★

The soul of Abercromby's host
Follows Lord Howe - his shining ghost;
On stormy ridge and parapet
It rides in flame, it leads them yet:
Smiling, with wistful image wan,
A dead man leads the dying on.
And Campbell, Laird of Inverawe,
Hath met the doom his dream foresaw;
Pierced by his murdered kinsman's eyes,
His clansmen bear him where he dies.
Lord Howe, Lord Howe, why shouldst thou fall!
Thy life, it was the life of all;
Thy death ten thousand hath undone.
England hath sunken with the sun.
Ticonderoga's lost, and won!

The Bridge, The Brigadier, and the Hill

Sources

1. Parkman, p. 385
2. Parkman, pp. 411-412
3. Ibid.
4. Lewis, p. 92
5. Roby, p. 39
6. Bougainville, pp. 104, 208, 209, 212
7. Bougainville, pp. 219-220; Loescher, *History*, p. 8
8. Bougainville, pp. 219-220
9. Bougainville, p. 224; *Documents Relating to the Colonial History of the State of New York* (Hereafter cited as *DRCHSNY*), Vol. X, pp. 790, 844
10. Loescher, *History*, p. 8; *DRCHSNY*, Vol. X, p. 894
11. Parkman, p. 414
12. Ibid.
13. Stark, p. 25
14. Bougainville, p. 226
15. Parkman, p. 415
16. Bougainville, p. 227; *DRCHSNY*, Vol. X, p. 738
17. Parkman, p. 415
18. Pouchot, p. 140; *DRCHSNY*, Vol. X, p. 722
19. Bougainville, p. 228
20. Cuneo, p. 85
21. *DRCHSNY*, Vol. X, p. 735
22. Parkman, p. 417
23. *DRCHSNY*, Vol. X, pp. 751, 895. Bougainville, p. 228
24. Lucier, Vol. III, p. 102
25. Pouchot, p. 141
26. Parkman, p. 360; *DRCHSNY*, Vol. X, p. 735
27. Bougainville, p. 229
28. Rutledge, *Century of Conflict*, p. 450
29. Richards, pp. 51-52

PART TWO

The Controversy

The Methods

In order to find the exact location of the battlesites, it was necessary to employ various methods. Over the years, many people have speculated about where the battles might have happened. This speculation can be likened to

(1) *conjecture*, [noun] —formation of an opinion on incomplete information, or

(2) *guess*, [noun] —an estimate without calculation or measurement.

Okay, we all have, and are entitled to, our own opinions—*opinion*, [noun] —unproved but probable belief. But to verify the sites of the battles, we had to go from opinion to certainty. *Certainty*, [noun] —undoubted fact. This we accomplished in three ways.

First, we examined descriptions of the battlesites found in the diaries and letters of participants. Plotting out the sites with an architectural compass on a topographical map, we were able to determine probable battle locations where the compass circles intersected and overlapped. But this still left us with a large area to explore, and the sites could be in any number of places. Two other authors and well-known Ranger buffs used this method to pick the spots where they believed the first battle on snowshoes could have happened. Unfortunately, both were wrong. Exhaustingly covering both locations with their metal detectors, Keith and Dan did not find a single piece of evidence or artifact at either place.

Narrowing down the large *possible* area into a more *probable* location became the second step, which was my specialty: recreating the time and distance according to first-person journal entries over exactly the same ground, in exactly the same weather conditions in exactly the same clothing, footgear and equipment—that is, snow-covered ground on snowshoes.

I have been hunting, guiding and period trekking in this area for over 20 years. When I started research for my first book, *The Battle on Snowshoes*, back in the early 1990's, I spent many hours and days trudging over and around the different paths, roads, trails and streets in the town of Ticonderoga that would have been traveled by French patrols and English raiding parties during the French and Indian War. I can assure the reader that I managed to raise quite a few eyebrows walking through the village in my 18th-century clothing, with snowshoes strapped to my feet and a musket over my shoulder.

But the good people of this town are used to seeing re-enactors, although usually in the summer months, so the novelty eventually wore off. As the years progressed, even to the research done on this book, now barely a glance is given to me anymore. When I stop for coffee and a meal at my favorite diner, The Hot Biscuit, the owners, Bonnie and Orley Dixon, my favorite waitress, Martha Blanchard, or the local customers just nod and ask, "Another book?" or, "Doing more research?"

The Trek

It was a cold, wintry day at about 9:30 a.m., when Keith dropped me off at Fivemile Point to begin my research trip of the Rangers' route of travel, according to contemporary journals and documents.

As Keith drove away, I went down to the shore of Lake Champlain near the very spot where Rogers and his Rangers lay waiting in ambush for the French sleighs.

In 1757, this point of land would have been thickly covered with trees to the water's edge. Today, it is very open, with some small trees and brush. Directly across the lake at this point is the eastern shore and the state of Vermont. Standing here, it doesn't take much imagination to transport you back to that overcast morning of January 21, 1757, when Rogers and Stark sprang the ambush.

Before I left this site, another thought crossed my mind. It was also at this exact spot, in February of 1760, that Rogers himself was ambushed, along with his new recruits and the payroll. How ironic that must have been, for the Major of all Ranging companies, to be caught off his guard at this favored ambush spot; and that by his nemesis, Langy de Montegron, the same man who also defeated him so devastatingly in the 1758 Battle on Snowshoes.

As I started back on my journey towards the Trout Brook Valley, with my *raquettes*, 18th-century compass, and flint and steel fire kit, I wondered just how close in time this trek would compare with that of the Ranger force in 1757. The distance would be almost exactly the same. But what about the time?

For one thing, this day had different weather conditions. It was very windy and cold, with the snow crusted and hard-packed; not like the drizzly January thaw in 1757. For me to try to duplicate this trip in a semblance of time to correspond to the Rangers, I would have to adjust my strides and speed.

As I traveled along over the landscape, I decided to enter the ravines created over the centuries by the waters of Fivemile Creek and follow them southwest into the Trout Brook Valley. After a mile or so of this, I came to a definite conclusion. The Rangers did NOT travel through these ravines, as some writers have suggested, for the following reasons:

1) Today, most of the land has been cleared into farms, open fields and pastures, so to avoid being seen, a person would need to travel in the ravines. However, in those days of two centuries ago, this was one immense forest, crowded with trees in every direction. Sight would be limited to about 60 yards or less. There simply would have been no need to conceal oneself in the ravine.

2.) Then, as now, ravines and draws are always choked with brush, blowdowns, and the thick, scrubby woods plants that always grow alongside watercourses, and make any kind of travel slow and laborious.

3.) Tactically speaking, being down in a ravine is a decided no-no, for it gives your enemy the advantage of the higher ground. I believe that they probably kept the ravines in close proximity and used them only for direction reference.

After about two hours and what I estimated to be about three miles, I came to a unique feature of land on my right side that made me stop and take notice. In military terms it was the perfect site for a camp. At this point, the Fivemile Creek itself was joined by two other brooks coming from the north and west. Before the three joined together, a high mound of land arose, shaped somewhat like a modern-day football. While I stood there gazing upon this unique feature, my stomach reminded me that it was hungry and thirsty, and this was as good a spot as any to stop and rest, and also kill approximately an hour to coincide with that period of time that the Rangers took to dry their guns (see p. 45). Climbing the knob from the southeast slope, I observed it to be approximately 100 yards by 200 yards in circumference, plenty of room for 74 men to camp in safety, with sentries out on the flanks. No chance of a surprise attack here.

Before I resume the description of my trek, I'd like to take a moment to reconstruct what probably transpired as the Rangers paused to dry their muskets.

Drying the Muskets

> *"...I gave orders to return with all possible expedition to our fires of the last encampment, in order to dry our guns, which we did effectually."* -Robert Rogers

> *"It being a rainy day, we made a fire and dry d our guns."* -Thomas Brown

In recreating the actions and movements of the past, it is essential to reckon time as accurately as possible in order to calculate the distances traveled. Based on my own experience with black powder firearms, and that of my trekking partners Fred Gowen, Dan Broderick and Mark Daiute, the following procedures were likely to have been performed by the Rangers as they dried their muskets.

Seventy-four Rangers and seven prisoners returned on the trail to the encampment of January 20, 1757. When they arrived at the site, one or more of the Rangers would have been ordered to stand guard over the prisoners. Next, several sentries would have been sent out to establish a defensive perimeter on the front, rear and sides of the camp. In the meantime some of the men would rekindle the coals, coaxing them into flames with pieces of birch bark and small twigs of pine, spruce, cedar and hemlock. As this was being done, other Rangers would be returning from a quick forage with armfuls of larger dry branches of wood, preferably from those limbs of trees above the wet ground.

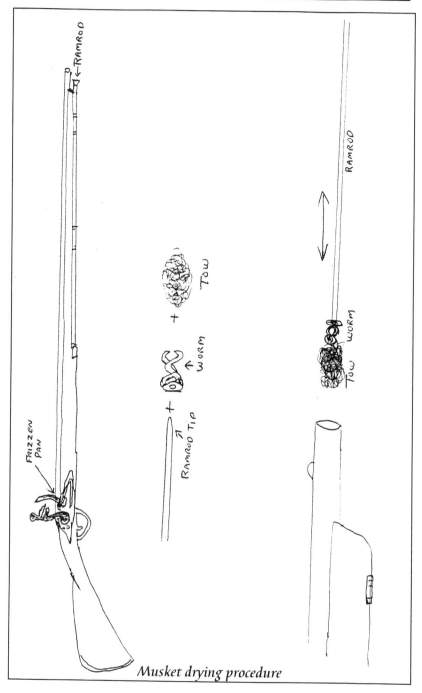

Musket drying procedure

Now, it stands to reason that 60 or more Rangers could not fit or work effectively around one campfire, so we think they probably divided into smaller, squad-sized groups of men around six to eight fires, thus keeping the drying time to a minimum. The statement, *"We made a fire and dry d our guns"* should not be interpreted casually by the reader. Sticking a musket loaded with black powder into a fire is not what was meant. This would be catastrophic, given the explosive nature of black powder.

What was done was this: each Ranger would have attached a worm (see drawing) to his ramrod, inserted it into the barrel of his gun and pulled out the wadding or paper cartridge. If the powder in his gun barrel came out dry, he would attach a piece of flaxen tow to the worm, run it in and out of the barrel to loosen any damp powder, wipe the lock of the frizzen pan of its priming residue, and then proceed to load with a fresh charge, taking care not to let any rain or snow get into the powder.

If a Ranger's powder charge was wet, he had no choice but to pull the charge, then pour water or melted snow down the barrel, and, working his ramrod with its tow-covered worm, flush and scrub the barrel until no evidence of powder was left. He would replace the wet tow with successive dry ones as often as necessary until the barrel appeared dry. He would then hold the barrel near enough to the fire to allow any remaining moisture to dissipate. Finally, he, too, was ready to re-load again fresh. As Fred Gowen states, cleaning a musket in a half-assed manner is as bad, or worse, than not cleaning it at all.

We figure that from the time the force of 74 men arrived at the campsite, re-started the fires, cleaned the muskets thoroughly, and went on their way, about 45 minutes to one hour would have elapsed.

For the reader's further enjoyment and education in eighteenth-century winter camping, I strongly recommend reading "A Typical Day's Journey in Winter," by Fred Gowen, in *The Book of Buckskinning VII*, Scurlock Publishing Co., Texarkana, Texas.

Now let's get back to the trek.

I took out my fire kit, gathered small twigs of spruce and pine, crumpled up some shredded birchbark, and struck my flint to the steel, sending a shower of sparks into the tow. Blowing gently a few times, I managed to coax the sparks into a glow that finally burst into the flame I wanted. Adding more bark and twigs, I soon had a hot fire going. After feeding the flames with gradually thicker pieces of wood, the fire was blazing sufficiently for my needs. I went down to the nearest stream and filled my brass kettle with cold water, and returned to the fire where I proceeded to brew up some tea. While waiting for the brew, I took out some of Holly's molasses ship's bread, and some venison jerky, made from the Cliff's buck taken last fall. While I sat there, fleeting thoughts raised questions in my mind. How close was I, really, to the actual site where Rogers and his men had camped and later returned to dry out the muskets? And if this was not the spot, which seemed to fit both time and distance, then where was it? The dancing flames and tendrils of aromatic woodsmoke gave no hints or answers today.

As the fire died down to a bed of coals, the sharpness of the wind seemed to increase. Reluctantly I stood up and heaped handfuls of crusted snow upon the remains of my fire, and then, satisfied that it was out, made ready to resume the trek. Shouldering my pack and fusil, I continued on towards the mountains that framed the valley of Trout Brook, very apparent in the narrowing distance. I arrived in town, sans my *raquettes*, and walked to the point of land where Trout Brook turns east and heads down the slope towards its junction with the waters of La Chute. Since leaving the site where I had taken my refreshment, I calculated covering between 1-1/2 and 2 miles. I took out my 18th-century sundial compass and reckoned the time at about 2:15 p.m.

Scanning the area, I realized that the location and the landscape matched up well with written accounts of the battles. Had I found the battlesite? Looking directly across Trout Brook, I saw the snow covered hillside and felt that somewhere, on that slope, time and distance could come together.

Now the final stage, the real proof of the pudding, was to see if Keith and Dan could verify the site by finding artifacts there. And verify it as a battlesite, they did, beyond any doubt. After securing permission from the landowners, Keith and Dan, using their metal detectors, uncovered a historian's dream: over 420 dropped musket balls of various caliber and shape, including almost 60 fired and deformed balls scattered in various patterns; buckshot, chewed balls, flints, broken gun parts, and locks of both French and English make. There were also coins, ice creepers, shoe buckles, tomahawks and knives, and many other artifacts that confirmed our theory— this was *definitely* the site of a furious battle, or perhaps two.

Now Keith Dolbeck will explain how he and Dan Blanchette do what they do best—uncover lost history to benefit us all.

Archeological Metal Detecting

Over the past several years, much ado has been made over the investigation of historical sites, or "relic hunting" with the use of metal detectors.

Archeological "purists" have maintained that history is being compromised by this other fraternity of history seekers who choose to use metal detectors to locate and investigate sites.

While I will agree that purists in any topical discussion often provide a necessary system of "checks and balances," they are not necessarily the last word on the subject.

Most fly fishermen will be quick to condemn the rod and reel spinner fisherman; and if you have ever cruised up to a yacht club with your seventy-five horse Johnson outboard, you can be assured of a lively discussion on the virtues of "sail versus sink" boating.

Every year, Fort Ticonderoga hosts a wonderful event called the "War College." Several experts are invited to share their French and Indian and Revolutionary War historical knowledge with the public as well as with each other. The author of this book has been invited to speak on two occasions.

After attending this event for several years, I was able to formulate some rather unique *opinions* of my own. Because the journals of the period are often sketchy at best with respect to battle and encampment locations, many of these alleged "documented" sites are purely *conjecture*. And those who have fully researched the period will readily admit this fact. Having been a teacher of science for almost thirty years in both the college and the public school system, I began to ask questions about the use of technology in the field of archeology. Could technology provide more conclusive *certainty* about the locations of such battlesites as "The Lord Howe Skirmish," the 1758 Battle on Snowshoes, and others? After all, we have put people on the moon, taken close up photographs of Mars, and exchanged several defective body parts for new ones. Should we continue to randomly dig archeological pits with spades and toothbrushes on a "hit or miss" basis to determine the historical importance of a piece of land? I don't think so!

Obviously there is much to be gained about a site by employing the more time-honored conventional methods of archeology, and I would never suggest abandoning them. But, if those methods were faster and more practical, there would not be as much *conjecture* or as many *opinions* as to where these locations actually exist. They would have been found by now.

Furthermore, what about possible historical sites that are becoming used for potential garages, swimming pools, housing developments, farming practices, etc.? On the grand scale of developing land, for example a shopping center, there are laws in New York state that require archeologists to dig *random* sites to determine the historical significance of the property. This is not done, however, on the personal property scale; and from the standpoint of people's landowner rights it probably should not be done.

In answer to the earlier question of technology in archeology, yes, there are scientifically based tools, which will help remove some of the aforementioned conjecture. They are called metal detectors. The ones my partner and I use, the White's Electronic Spectrum model XLT, are so sophisticated that, after several years' experience, we can often determine what is in the ground without ever having to dig. And we have documented several battlesites, such as the topic of this book, that over the past two hundred and fifty years have remained anonymous.

Once the decision was made to incorporate the use of metal detectors in our pursuit of eighteenth century history, we needed to establish some guidelines or archeologically acceptable methods for documenting a found site. Obviously, we should seek out archeologists specializing in the period and receive some lessons on methodology. This we did; and while we were perceived as "radicals" in the field, we were given cordial treatment.

For the sake of easier reading, I will outline our methodology in steps.

Step 1

Research, research, research! For this particular site that is the subject of this book I read the journal and orderly book of Captain Monypenny, aid to Lord George Augustus Viscount Howe; Robert Rogers' after action reports; personal diary of Thomas Brown, corpsman of Rogers Rangers, and many others.

Step 2

Once an area has been chosen as a possible site and permission of the landowner has been gained, a series of patterns are established. We sweep the area to locate any and all metals. When we locate a target, we carefully dig the target and mark the location with a flag. If the target is not a period artifact, for example a tractor part, a shell casing, or some other identifiable metal object, we remove it, replace the sod, and continue our search.

If the target is a period artifact such as a brass gun part, King George farthing coin, or a musket ball, we re-establish our search pattern to one much smaller and tighter in control. At that point we take a reading with a global positioning satellite (GPS) compass and obtain a latitude and longitude reading for that area.

We then continue to sweep the area; and if that particular spot seems to yield a significant (usually greater than five) number of period artifacts, we will carefully dig a small pit and examine the area for non-metallic artifacts such as shards of glass, pottery and clay, as well as gun flints, etc.

In some cases our area may encompass someone's manicured lawn; and while we can carefully remove an artifact and replace a sod plug, the landowner might request that no further excavations be done. In these cases no archeology could be done without metal detectors.

Step 3

All artifacts removed from the site are identified and logged either onto a computer database or in field notes. Pertinent information such as identity, placement, depth, type of soil, position of the artifact, and condition of the artifact are all noted. There are many good identification reference materials. We use the *Collector's Illustrated Encyclopedia of the American Revolution* by George C. Neumann and Frank J. Kravic and *History Written With Pick and Shovel* by William L. Calver and Reginald P. Bolton. We have also become somewhat expert on the identification of French and Indian and Revolutionary War artifacts. My partner and I would certainly be available to help anyone with the identification of a period artifact.

Step 4

Photographs are taken of the area. We try to take as much an aerial view as possible. We then enlarge the photograph by computer enhancement and grid the site. Each grid square is lettered, and each artifact is given a number and its position where found is placed on the grid.

Step 5

Preservation of the artifacts. We carefully soak and clean each artifact with a fine soft toothbrush and then preserve it depending on its metallic content. Pewter buttons, for example, should be routinely coated with petroleum jelly to prevent them from flaking. Iron objects are cleaned and either coated with chemicals to prevent further oxidation or waxed for the same purpose. Silver artifacts do not need much attention. Once the artifacts are preserved, they are catalogued and placed in glass-covered specimen cases. Each case only contains artifacts from one particular site.

After these steps are taken, the artifacts and their photos are used for slide shows and school education programs and are available by appointment for authors and historians to use to further the pursuits of eighteenth century history.

Remember that some historical properties like Fort Ticonderoga have been set aside for the expressed purpose of interpreting and researching history. These associations have the means, expertise and purpose to provide for archeological digs. These areas should not be investigated with metal detectors, and it is in fact against the law to do so.

Written by Keith Dolbeck
7/4/99

1757 Snow Ambush Site

We knew from the preponderance of artifacts found that we had undoubtedly discovered the site of a battle, but which one—the January 21, 1757, ambush on snowshoes, or the July 6, 1758, death of Lord Howe? Let's look at the sources to give us the clues.

The French accounts of the January 21, 1757, battle are as follows: On February 1, 1757, Bougainville wrote in his journal, "At noon a courier arrived from Carillon who brought us word of an affair which took place two leagues from the fort on January 21."[1] (How far is a league? Dictionary definitions range from 2.4 to 4.6 statute miles. With Fivemile Point as our reference, we concluded that two leagues are approximately equal to five miles.)

An anonymous account sent to France states, "About 3 o'clock in the afternoon this party halted and waited for the English, within 3 leagues of Fort Carillon."[2]

Referring back to our first chapter, the French officer who acted as the interpreter when Private Thomas Brown was taken prisoner stated that Brown "should have relief when I came to Ticonderoga, which was but one mile and a 1/4 off."[3]

Finally, Captain de Hebecourt of the Regiment La Reine stated in his after action report that followed the March 13, 1758, Battle on Snowshoes, where Rogers' Rangers were decimated by Langy, that "this affair took place on the 13th in the evening, at about the same place as that of January 21st last year."[4]

"At about the same place" is a vague measurement and makes one wonder. The battlesite this book concerns itself with lies northeast of the 1758 Battle on Snowshoes site by about one mile.

To sum up the French accounts of the distance between Carillon and the battlesite: one source says two leagues, another claims three leagues (big difference), Brown said his captor told him "one mile and 1/4 off", and Capt. de Hebecourt stated "At about the same place as last year." Not exactly pinpoint directions, are they?

Now let's look at the English accounts found in Robert Rogers' and Private Thomas Brown's journals—the only two first-person accounts—and see how they intersect with the site locations given in the French sources.

Rogers stated that he made camp the night of January 20, 1757, "on the west side, three miles from Lake Champlain."[5] After his ambush of the sleighs, he returned to the previous evening's campsite, re-kindled his fires, dried the muskets, and headed hurriedly towards home. He then stated, "In this manner, we advanced *half a mile* over broken ground."[6]

Private Thomas Brown recorded that after drying his musket, "We proceeded in this order about *a mile and a half.*"[7] —Another big difference between distance estimates.

Having conducted my own 18th-century trekking research of the site, and, based on where the artifacts were found, I tend to agree more with Brown's estimate, and I feel that he is probably even shy by 1/3 to 1/2 of a mile. So why is there such a discrepancy in the accounts of Rogers and Brown? After all, they were in exactly the same place at the same time. Remember that Rogers, being the leader, had a lot more on his mind. Also, it must be remembered that Rogers took a grazing ball to the head at the onset of the battle. This, along with not writing the account until weeks later, would naturally make his confusion understandable.

Rogers' actual description of the battlesite location says that they were "crossing a valley between two very steep hills, which was about 15 rods wide; when the front to the number of 10 or 12 had raised the summit on the western side, a volley of two hundred shots or there about was fired upon us ..."[8]

Brown's account gives a more detailed description of the entire site. He mentions that during the battle he saw a large rock which he decided to hide behind until meeting an Indian coming out from the other side, who then threw his tomahawk at Brown.[9] Later on in the evening, after being abandoned by Rogers, Brown, wounded, crawls to the fire where Speakman and Kennedy are sitting; and he notices "an Indian coming towards us over a small rivulet that parted us in the engagement."[10]

Brown then tries desperately to escape the rest of the evening by crawling through the snow. "But the snow and cold put my feet into such pain, as I had no shoes, that I could not go on. I therefore sat down by a brook."[11] (Obviously different than the aforementioned rivulet.)

Finally, on the next morning, when perhaps the visibility was clearer, Brown says, "I heard the shouts of Indians behind me, and I supposed they saw me; within a few minutes four came running down a mountain, running towards me."[12]

Having thoroughly investigated the site, I can tell the reader that there is a valley of an estimated fifteen rods width, with the first hill (which would be that of Stark's covering position) being the higher of the two. There is a small rivulet at the scene, a brook perhaps 1/3 of a mile away, and there are large boulders off to the side. It is at the base of Bear Mountain, which is the only mountain in the vicinity, and if Brown had crawled towards the east all night long when taken prisoner the next day by the four Indians coming off of the mountain, he would have been moving closer to the fort (but still farther than the French officer's estimate of 1 and 1/4 mile). Also, what is obvious to the researcher is that Brown knew the difference between a rivulet and a brook, and a hill and a mountain.

Taken together, both Rogers' and Brown's accounts fit the site perfectly, except for one point. Rogers stated that "the front of his force having gained the summit of the opposite hill on the west side."[13] The opposite hill in this site is on the SOUTH side (see Map A, p. 3). So are we in the wrong place? Maybe. Maybe not.

Why did Rogers say that this hill was on the western slope? The day was extremely overcast and rainy with no sunshine. Was he really concerned about the hill's location? Did he have a compass in his hand at that moment? Did the musket ball that whacked him in the forehead confuse his memory? Maybe. Maybe not.

Maybe Rogers intentionally wrote "west" to give the impression that he headed back toward the Trout Brook Valley instead of taking a quicker and shorter route to the lake. While this theory may be speculation, there is ample reason not to take Robert Rogers' words as gospel. He had a habit of not being altogether truthful in his reports and also leaving out information that might be damaging to him at a later date. Let me explain.

Robert Rogers was a great self promoter. He embellished his victories and downplayed his defeats by the juggling of enemy numbers. Case in point—After his near annihilation by Langy in the 1758 Battle on Snowshoes, he reported that the enemy force was "700, of which 600 were Indians."[14] The ACTUAL number of the French and Indian force was 301. Matching that against the Rangers' force of 183 doesn't even make the odds two to one. When taking into consideration that Rogers and his men were hidden in ambush and held the higher ground, and claimed to have killed "above 40 Indians" at the outset,[15] Rogers definitely had no reason to have been beaten so soundly. Consequently, his reports had to make it appear that he was outnumbered and overwhelmed by sheer numbers of the enemy. Another case in point—After destroying the Abenaki village of St. Francis, Rogers claims to have killed "above 200 Indians."[16] Modern-day evidence places the total killed at less than forty and many of these possibly were women and children.[17] Captain Pierre Pouchot recalled in his memoirs that Robert Rogers "found this Abenaki village entirely denuded of its warriors. He killed around thirty women and old people and brought back a number of young men prisoner."[18]

Just as obvious as his inflation of figures is Rogers' reluctance to tell or admit to all the facts. After one particularly devastating ambush by partisan leader St. Luc de La Corne near Half-way Brook, General Abercromby dispatched a force of 700 men to sweep the area around South Bay clear of enemy forces.[19] Failing to catch or encounter these raiders, Rogers and his combined force of Rangers and provincials made camp near the ruins of old Fort Anne on Wood Creek. The next morning, relaxing all military caution, Rogers engaged in a marksmanship duel with Ens. William Irwin, a volunteer from Gage's regulars.[20]

The shots reached the ears of the French partisan leader, Joseph Marin, who was not far away with a smaller force. Marin set an ambush at the head of a clearing that he knew the Rangers would go through on their way back to Fort Edward. As the English column started into the forest, the trap was sprung. The lead men, including Israel Putnam, Lieutenant Tracy, and three Connecticut provincials, were seized and taken prisoner. Firing then erupted, driving the English force back and strewing the ground with dead and wounded. The British regrouped under Rogers' orders and began to flank the French, eventually driving the smaller force away. More than forty of Rogers' men were killed, and at least that many were wounded.[21]

Even though he killed as many of the enemy and retained the field of battle, Rogers' lack of judgment in firing at marks was not forgotten or forgiven by the Connecticut men who suffered the greatest number of casualties because of it.

Rogers never 'fessed up to his mistake and never mentioned it in any official report, but it was recorded by others.

Here is what the Rev. John Cleaveland says in his diary: "August 9, 1758. Wednesday. This evening heard that Major Rogers and Major Putnam have had a brush with the French and Indians at Wood Creek near Fort Anne: that our men were marching in an Indian file, that Major Rogers and a regular Officer in the front were firing at marks upon a wager..."[22]

"11 August. Friday. ...and that they had the advantage of us by hearing our men firing at marks in the morning. This is a judgement of God upon us."[23]

Finally, "August 13. Sabbath. ...Captain Giddings, who went out with Rogers returned to camp this afternoon and says that the Officers did fire at marks the morning before the fight..."[24]

Rogers' erroneous facts and figures in many of his reports, and his omission of certain information, make his journals somewhat questionable. Because of this, I tend to wonder about the veracity or accuracy of his description of the "western hill." He could very well be mistaken or perhaps was purposely misleading his superiors. But I believe that he simply was mistaken. The route of travel at this site would be south, not west. By heading this way (south) he would arrive at Lake George much sooner, it being less than two miles away. Once on the ice, he could take off the snowshoes and speed homeward safely without fear of an ambush. By heading into the Trout Brook Valley, he would be forced to go another five to six miles on snowshoes before he reached Lake George.

Now let's examine how the evidence points to the probability that Lord Howe met his death at this same place.

1757 Site Location

Sources

1. Bougainville, pp. 80-81
2. Loescher, *History*, p. 347
3. Loescher, *History*, p. 334
4. Loescher, *History*, p. 387
5. Roby, p. 28
6. Roby, p. 29
7. Loescher, *History*, p. 332
8. Loescher, *History*, p. 326
9. Loescher, *History*, p. 332
10. Loescher, *History*, p. 136
11. Loescher, *History*, p. 333
12. Ibid.
13. Roby, p. 29
14. Roby, p. 53
15. Roby, p. 50
16. Loescher, *Genesis*, pp. 56-65
17. Day, p. 16
18. Pouchot, p. 249
19. Loescher, *Genesis*, p. 16
20. Loescher, *Genesis*, p. 17
21. Loescher, *Genesis*, pp. 19-20
22. Cleaveland, p. 209
23. Cleaveland, p. 210
24. Cleaveland, p. 211

1758 Lord Howe Site

As the British army landed at dawn on July 6, 1758, there happened an event, small at the time but later to become the determining factor and subsequent reason for Abercromby's defeat and the death of Lord Howe.

Despite their best efforts to anticipate and block the landings, the French were caught by surprise. Realizing that to stay and fight would be tantamount to suicide, they effected a military withdrawal, destroying the river bridges and therefore denying the British a swift and easy route to the fort.

Not much is mentioned about *how* the French destroyed the bridges. With absence of any noted "explosion" by either side's reports, one is left to wonder how it was done. Bougainville states, "Sieur de Bourlamaque retreated in good order and without losing a single man, although in the presence of the enemy. He joined up with the Marquis de Montcalm, and five reunited battalions crossed the river of the falls, destroying the bridge."[1]

Cuneo writes, "The French, apparently caught by surprise, fled in confusion from their posts on the western shore across the bridge to the portage road. All they could do of value was to destroy the bridge after themselves."[2]

But the Reverend John Cleaveland makes it clear in his journal just how the bridge was destroyed:

"...for though the enemy had four battalions in ye advance guard and several cannon, yet by nine o'clock in ye morning we were all safely landed; the French only fired a few small arms which did no harm and then run off. But as they Burnt the bridges over the river, the army marched through the thick woods to go round ye bend of ye river, and when we marched about two miles we were attacked."[3]

Another entry states,

"Here the troops formed in four columns, and began the advance, without however, their artillery and heavy baggage, which had to be left behind until the bridges, which had been burned by the advance guard of the enemy, in their retreat, could be rebuilt."[4]

With the destruction of the bridge, the British were faced with a choice—seize the ground and rebuild the bridge or press on along the west side of La Chute which would bring them to Ticonderoga without ever having to cross the river. In order to save time the British pressed onward through the forest with Lord Howe leading the way.

The forest was gloomy and primeval; towering trees blocked out the sun and gave midday the appearance of dusk. Vines, boulders, deadfalls, and huge decaying stumps formed an obstacle course for mile after mile. Fetid swamps with cattails, ferns, and rushes fed by small streams and brooks became quagmires as thousands of marching feet churned through them. Mosquitoes, black flies, and deer flies rose off the dampness by the thousands to attack any exposed skin, and the heat became suffocating, like that of a sweat lodge. This slow, maddening march headed toward the site where young Lord Howe's life would be sacrificed to the gods of war.

But where exactly was that site? Local tradition throughout the 1800's and 1900's suggested that the battle took place near the present site of St. Mary's cemetery. In the late 1700's James Madison and Thomas Jefferson toured the area and asked to be shown the site where Lord Howe had fallen. Standing near the upper falls, they were told that it was west of them up on the hill.

In the latter half of the twentieth century, a historical sign was erected by the American Legion Post 224. It is located between Lord Howe Street and La Chute River in the modern village of Ticonderoga. It says, "DEATH OF LORD HOWE, Near this spot, July 6, 1758, Lord George Augustus Viscount Howe was killed in a skirmish preceding Abercromby's defeat by Montcalm at Fort Carillon."

As for location from written sources, Edward P. Hamilton states, "After advancing a mile or so the British floundered into contact with a French detachment also gone astray."[5]

Another source states that, "At 2 o'clock in the afternoon, all the regiments except three, advanced to take possession of the favorable posts on the height near the saw mill, one mile and a half from Carillon. At 4 o'clock they fell in with 350 French on the hill halfway between the landing place and the mill."[6]

Rev. John Cleaveland notes in his journal, "The army marched thro the thick woods to go round ye bend of ye river and when we had marched about two miles, we were attacked in ye front..."[7] Bougainville records, "However the 350 man detachment which Sieur de Langy led abandoned by the few Indians who served it as guides, went astray in the mountains and after 12 hours marching came into contact with an English column which was proceeding towards the Bernetz river."[8] Trout Brook, called by the French the Bernes or Bernetz River, joins the La Chute River (or Ticonderoga Creek) from the west between upper and lower La Chute falls. The creek was named in 1756 for Chevalier de Bernetz, commandant of the Royal Roussillon Battalion.[9]

So here we have sources which tell us that approximately "a mile or so," "about two miles," "proceeding towards the Bernetz river," and "on the hill, halfway between the landing place and the mill."

The English entries make it fairly clear as to direction, but distance estimates vary. However, "on the hill" makes the picture a lot sharper. When we find the French detachment near the "Bernetz river," the area we look for becomes narrowed down. (See Map B.)

Here I would like to pause for a moment and share my thoughts concerning the "lost" French detachment that unknowingly caused history to take an unexpected turn. A lot of the history books we read allude to the statement that Langy and Trépezec and their command were "lost." I'm not sure I buy that. Langy was the ultimate scout, the master woodsman; every bit equal to Robert Rogers. He was very familiar with this area. Less than four months earlier he had decimated Rogers and his Rangers at the Battle on Snowshoes in the Trout Brook Valley. In July of 1757 he had helped lead Chevalier de Levis and the land force of Montcalm's army through the Trout Brook Valley, *Route des Agniers, Les Arbres Mataches,* or Mohawk Trail—whatever you prefer to call it.

Les Arbre Mataches is described as the "war painted" trees in Hamilton's translation of Bougainville's journal, so the trail would seem to have taken its name from the way in which it was marked. It ran from Carillon to Ganaouske (Northwest) Bay and then on to the south end of Lake George. It was situated behind the mountains on the west side of the lake. The route was used successfully by Levis' corps of Montcalm's army on its journey to attack and destroy Fort William Henry, and is shown beginning at the Bernetz River on a map of Lake George and southern Lake Champlain in Thomas Mante's 1772 work, *The History of the Late War in North-America and the Islands of the West-Indies.*[10] Langy also knew this route and the locations of different patrol trails that

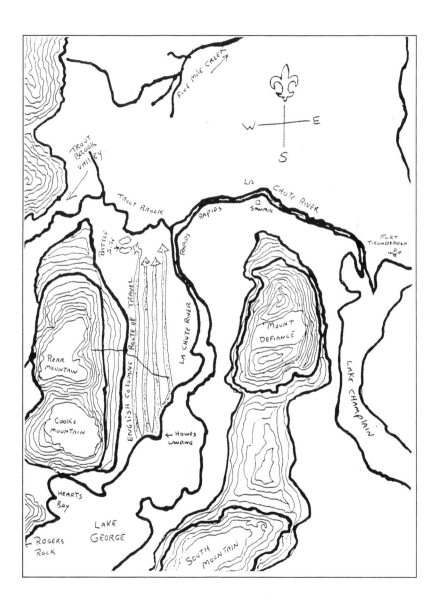

Area of battle in which Lord Howe was killed. (Map B.)

wound through these hills. On the very day before the skirmish with Lord Howe, Langy had led a detachment up to Mont Pélée (Rogers' Rock) and back. Bougainville recorded, "Detachment sent to Pélée Mountain returned without having seen anything."[11]

Okay, for the sake of argument, it is apparent that whatever route Langy and Trépezec took to their position on the evening of July 5, they either could not, or chose not, to take the same route back to Carillon. That seems obvious. It is also obvious that to avoid the British army, which had already landed and placed themselves between the French detachment and Fort Carillon, the easiest and safest way to return would be to take the patrol trail that followed the ravine between Rogers' Rock and Cook's Mountain to Trout Brook, which would lead back to Carillon. Being woodsmen, they knew that ALL the waters, be they brooks, rivulets, streams, creeks, or whatever, eventually flowed into Trout Brook or Lake George, both of which became the waters of La Chute, which emptied into Lake Champlain under the guns of Carillon. This knowledge alone would prevent anyone from getting "lost" from the fort. It is not improbable that one or more of the officers may have had a compass. If not, they would have used the position of the sun, rising in the east and setting in the west, to give them not only an idea of direction but also of time. Finally, all woodsmen are aware that moss grows heaviest on the north side of trees.

Enough of the point is made here. These men knew which way to go back to the fort even if they were not on a beaten path.

But why did it take them 12 hours, as some have suggested, to get back? And why were they "abandoned by their Indian guides"?

It is recorded that there were only about 15 Indians available to the French prior to the battle of Carillon.[12] Now, my question is this: If you were an Indian, allied to the

French, courted and showered with foods and gifts, why would you "abandon" the party you were asked to guide? How do you explain "losing" your party when you return to the fort? What could happen to make you decide to "abandon" your allies?

Keith Dolbeck has put forth an interesting theory. He believes that Langy and Trépezec, knowing they were unable to prevent the landing, instead of following the patrol trail back to the fort decided to cross from Mont Pélée over to Cook's and Bear Mountains, thus being able to see down to the lake and try to observe the movements of the British army. By staying on the top it is a simple matter to follow the crests of both mountains to the north end of Bear Mountain which will descend down to the hill which lies above Trout Brook and thence to the fort. Okay, that's reasonable. But why the "abandonment" by the Indians?

Here is another theory: Trépezec's direct orders from Montcalm were to "proceed as far as Mont Pélée and resist with all his might any troops who might come across country, as we supposed they would."[13] Now my question is, What did these direct orders mean to Trépezec? What sort of a man or commander was he? Was he an unquestioning robot? A sort of military zealot? Was he like George Armstrong Custer, the kind of man who would use or misuse orders to gain a bit of glory? What was going on in his mind? Just getting back to the fort, or maybe something else?

Is it completely out of the question to wonder if Trépezec and Langy held council to talk and urge their men to perhaps lay an ambush and take a piece out of the British advance? Did they also exhort the Indians to fight beside them, as did Captain Daniel de Beaujeau at Fort Duquesne, prior to the resounding defeat of Braddock's army on the Monongahela?

And while this council is being held, what do the Indians think? No doubt they were not educated in the European complexities of math and addition, subtraction, and multiplication with figures. But their common sense and native wariness could tell them easily that the 15,000-man force below was a LOT bigger than their own group of 350. If the appeals and objections of the Indians were not listened to, or were ignored by the French, the natives might have said words among themselves such as "These white boys are crazy," "They look to sacrifice themselves and us," and "Let's get out of here." So either they stalked away in a group, or, what is more likely, simply melted into the forest one by one as the detachment struggled through the mountains.

Over time, fatigue will alter men's personalities. Scarcity of food, lack of cool, refreshing water, physical exertion, and the constant stress of combat conditions, weigh heavily upon soldiers and bring them to exhaustion quickly.

The French detachment was experiencing this. Thirsty for fresh water, carrying scant rations for the scout, and now abandoned by their Indian guides, the men became victims of the specter of fatigue. Even the shared command of Trépezec, the captain from the Bearn Regiment, and Langy, the famous ensign of the Canadian forests, seemed taut and strained.

After trudging across the rocky, treacherous mountains, it was indeed a welcome relief to finally cross on to the northern end of Bear Mountain, where the hillside sloped gradually eastward to the Bernetz and La Chute Rivers. The anticipation of the cool, rushing waters, and the knowledge that across the river was the army of Montcalm, and safety, brought renewed hope and vigor to the detachment. Little did these men know that they were about to engage in what would become one of history's most famous battles.

Although accounts of the battles seldom agreed, we finally were able to ascertain the battlesite location, and one thing is for certain: the artifacts found there tell us that *two* battles occurred here—one in winter, and one in summer.

Lord Howe Site

Sources

1. Bougainville, p. 227
2. Cuneo, p. 84
3. Cleaveland, p. 198
4. Society of Colonial Wars in the State of New York, p. 74
5. Hamilton, p. 219
6. *DRCHSNY*, Vol. X, p. 735
7. Cleaveland, p. 198
8. Bougainville, p. 228
9. Pouchot, pp. 140, 346
10. Ibid., pp. 346-347
11. Bougainville, p. 225
12. *DRCHSNY*, p. 738
13. Pouchot, p. 140

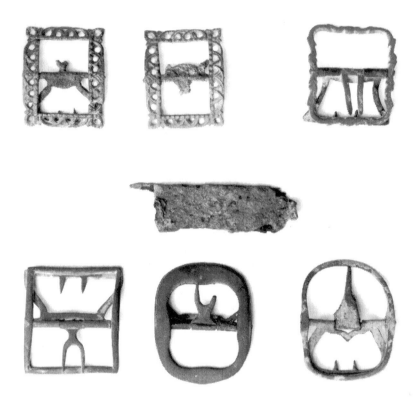

Top, l-r: Pair of French-style shoe buckles; single shoe buckle
Center: Single ice creeper
Bottom: English shoe buckles (middle with hallmark)
Extreme right buckle with "field repair," showing value of
such an item in the New World.

The Artifacts

Now it is time to let the artifacts tell us what happened at this location.

Ice Creepers

The function of ice creepers, used with shoes or moccasins, was to provide traction on icy surfaces in winter. Obviously, a Ranger would be unlikely to carry a pair of these on a summer campaign. A great discovery, two separate pairs of ice creepers were found at different locations in the battlesite area, indicating the probability of a winter battle.

Buckles

The significant number of pairs of buckles in good, serviceable condition lends support to the claim that this was the site of a fight and not a camp. Buckles were a very important commodity to the wearer and were not discarded unless broken and useless. In the photo at left we see a buckle that was obviously repaired by the owner. This suggests two things: 1, buckles were expensive and/or hard to come by, hence the need for repair: and 2, perhaps this was more likely to belong to an enlisted man, because an officer might have had the money and means to procure a new set.

Battlesite Artifact List

420 musket balls
1 lead pencil
1 rifleman's ax (square-
    pole hatchet)
1 candlestick holder
2 pairs ice creepers
1/2 ox shoe
7 complete shoe buckles
    (one identical pair)
5 incomplete buckles
11 shoe buckle fragments
2 complete knee buckles
3 incomplete knee buckles
1 complete shoulder strap
    buckle
3 incomplete shoulder
    strap buckles
1 cartridge box buckle
5 small equipment buckles
1 bayonet fragment
17 vented hollow
    undecorated buttons
3 large tombac coat
    buttons
8 various clothing buttons
    (decorated and
    undecorated)
2 English gun flints
2 French gun flints
3 finial bayonet scabbard
    tips

2 ramrod tips
1 large knife blade (French
    / Spanish blade)
1 complete pocket knife
    (English)
1 religious medal
1 campaign medal of
    unknown origin
3 large pewter spoons
1 large spoon handle
2 small spoon bowl
    fragments
5 bayonet scabbard frogs
1 cob (silver coinage)
11 King George Coppers
5 small pieces of brass gun
    furniture
1 two-prong fork (iron)
1 pair of sling swivels
    (iron)
1 brass front musket sight
1 iron frizzen
1 frizzen feather spring
1 iron sling band with
    swivel attached
1 belt ax (round eye)
1 ramrod guide
1 brass repair for the all
    too common break in
    the wrist of stock

Compiled by Dan Blanchette and Keith Dolbeck

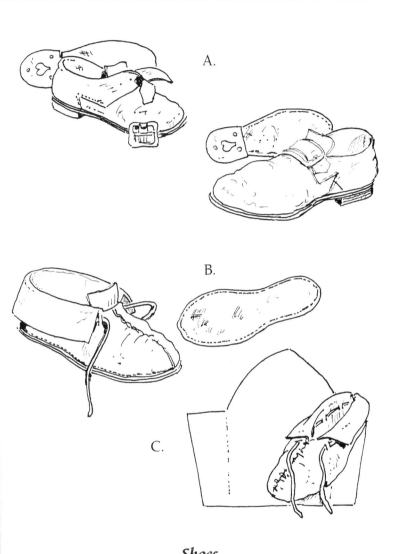

Shoes

A. Single-soled shoe
B. Double-soled variety for cold weather (Gallup and Shaffer, *La Marine*, p. 66.)
C. Center-seam style moccasin, of Iroquoian design, favored by rangers and English woods troops.

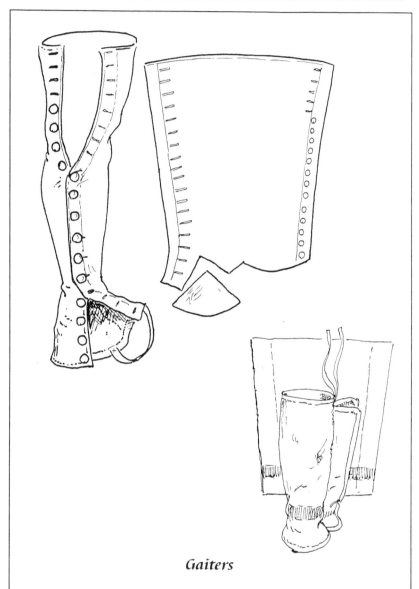

Gaiters

Called *guetres* by the French. They were made of a strong weave of cotton cloth similar to that of canvas. Used with breeches to protect the legs from brush, and would also help keep snow out of shoes and moccasins when laced underneath. They served the same purpose as would leggings.

Moccasins and liners

A. High-top style deerskin moccasins. Also known in French as
   souliers de chevreuil. This was the favored winter footwear of the
   French and Indian woodsmen of early North America.
B. Liners for the winter moccasin. Made out of blanket wool pieces
   sewn together. These were called *nipes* in French. Wool slippers
   that were made in one piece of wool or felt were called
   chaussons.

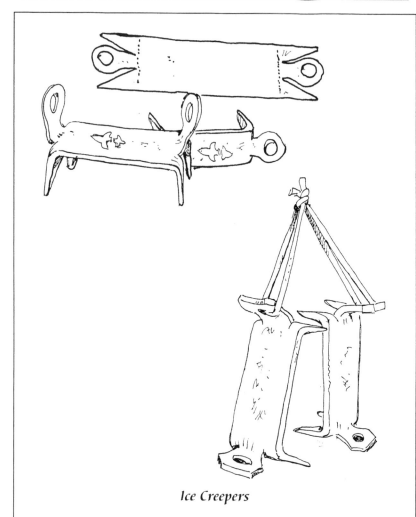

Ice Creepers

Called by the French, *grappins*. "Ice creepers are flat metal bars cut and bent at each end to provide two downward pointing prongs (to bite into the ice) and one flange, bent up, which was drilled or punched so a leather thong could tie the creeper to the shoe. (Stone 1974:83, 86) A specimen stamped with a fleur de lis is in the collection of Louisbourg. (Neumann and Kravic 1975:162). The English, while occupying Quebec during the winter of 1759-1760, issued ice-creepers from captured stores (Knox 1980:231). Gallup and Shaffer, *La Marine*, p. 129.

The large amount of buckles, especially those of matching pairs, leads to the following question: If the wearers of these were killed, how come the shoes with buckles were not taken for booty? Perhaps because the shoes were lost before the wearers died. But which is more likely: to lose one's footwear in the thickness of the summer forests, or in the deep snows of winter?

The answer to this at first glance would appear easy. Shoes were probably worn in the summer and moderate weather months, and boots or high moccasins in the winter. But Thomas Brown in his account of the winter battle used the word "shoes" four separate times. Surely he knew the difference between a shoe and a moccasin. "...I broke my snowshoes, I had time to pull em off, but was obliged to let my shoes go with them." "I found one of our people dead; I pulled off his stockings (he had no shoes) and put them on my own legs." "But as the snow and cold put my feet into such pain, as I had no shoes, that I could not go on." "I beg'd for a pair of shoes, and something to eat."[1]

Okay, it looks like shoes were used in the snowshoe fight. But wait a moment. Further research leads us to another possible conclusion. Maybe Brown meant "Indian shoes," a term which was commonly used in those days. "Some men also bought or fashioned Indian shoes (moccasins) and many officers wore boots, resembling riding boots of today."[2] "...moggosan or Indian slipper (moccasin, mockasin, molkasin, morgisson, mogashen, mackassin, mocsen); in the New Hampshire provincial papers of 1704 the spelling is mockasin."[3] So it would appear that the shoes Brown talks of are probably moccasins, or "Indian shoes."

This starts to make sense—until we wonder about the records that give credence to the use of shoes in cold weather, "The ship *Machault* sank in 1760 carrying military supplies for the soldiers in New France. The cargo included 500 pairs of shoes. These shoes are the typical square-toed buckled shoes of the eighteenth century. The French shoes were made with double and single soles, the double-soled variety for cold climates."[4]

As a counterpoint to the use of "shoes" in winter, let's look to the journal of British Captain John Knox, stationed in Quebec City in the winter of 1759-60, following the Battle on the Plains of Abraham. "Our soldiers make great progress in walking on snowshoes, but men not accustomed to them find them very fatiguing...; the hard-soled shoe is not at all suitable to them; they must be used under moggosans, as well as for the sake of the wearer's feet, to keep them warm and preserve them from the snow."[5]

So were shoes actually used with snowshoes in 1757? Maybe, maybe not. Knox seems to suggest in 1759 that it was felt that the use of shoes with snowshoes was "not at all suitable" and the wearer risked the danger of frostbite to his feet. But when and how did Knox and others learn this and come to that conclusion? Was it because of the earlier years of scouting experiences from, say, 1755 to 1757? It seems likely.

So we again are left to wonder. Are these shoe and buckle artifacts from the French and English soldiers engaged in the battle that took the life of Lord Howe in the summer of 1758? Or, could they be the shoes issued to the French troops who accompanied Langlade to the ambush in the snow in January of 1757? Remember, Bougainville stated "Our soldiers, who had no snowshoes, fought at a disadvantage, floundering in the snow up to their knees."[6] Or could they be the shoes of Thomas Brown and his Ranger comrades? "At Albany on September 17, 1756, the two Captains [Speakman and Hobbs] took an order from Abercrombie to Oliver DeLancey, an agent of Baker & Kilby, to supply them with 11 camp kettles and 62 canteens with ropes. The same day DeLancey delivered Speakman 36 pair of shoes, and Hobbs 30 pair. These shoes were the regulation army shoes."[7]

Brown was in Speakman's company.

Bullets

Most of the artifacts recovered from the battlesite are bullets—of both French and British calibers—some dropped, many fired: buckshot, split shot, chewed musket balls, and even rifled musket balls. Many readers will be puzzled to read of rifled balls (see photo, p. 83) being used as early as the French and Indian War. The common misconception is that rifles only started being used in the years of the American Revolution, and that smoothbore muskets were the only weapons used until then. However, rifles go back in history a long time, a VERY long time. The first ever evidence we have of a rifle is the one that belonged to Hapsburg ruler Maximilian I (1459-1519). This rifle has survived through the centuries, minus its lock, which was probably a snapping matchlock. The barrel is bronze instead of iron, fitted with a peep sight for better accuracy, and has a barrel rifled with 12 grooves in a slow twist.[8]

The first surviving record of a prize shooting with arquebuses dates from 1426, and as early as 1472 the practical Swiss held an all-gun meet. Usually these guns were smoothbores. For many years after the first rifles appeared they remained comparatively rare weapons. But their performance was so much better than the smoothbored pieces that mixed contests would have been unfair. Thus, these rifles were usually banned or, upon consent, regulated to special all-rifle matches. After 1560 such special classes became more and more common until by 1600 they were standard. At Basle in 1605 there was a dual meet. Smoothbores competed at 570 feet at a 2 ½ foot target while rifles were assigned the range of 805 feet at a 3 ½ foot target.[9]

The military potential of the rifle was slow to be recognized. King Christian IV of Denmark is generally considered to be the first European monarch to equip troops with a rifle early in the seventeenth century. Soon after, the French Royal Horse Guards boasted eight rifled carbines per cavalry troop.[10]

As immigrants of German descent came to America, they brought with them the knowledge and means to produce rifles similar to the "Jaeger" style from the homeland. These usually were deep multi-grooved barrels, between three and four feet in length (shorter than the later-evolving Kentucky/Pennsylvania rifles) with calibers around .70 to .75.

As to the use of the rifle in the French and Indian War, we have these sources. "Here in 1758, however, we find the rifle an article of issue, on a small scale to be sure, only 10 per regiment, but an official issue to British regulars. The expedition against Fort Duquesne that same summer also received a few. Some open-minded British officer, and he must have had powerful friends in the war office, had evidently been much impressed with the American rifle as used along the Pennsylvania frontier, and had taken one home. A considerable number were now made in England, following the American design exactly, and they now appeared in the hands of some of the troops in the campaign of 1758."[11]

"Abercromby and Howe had made their first major error; they expected Gage's light infantry and special units of the best marksmen of each regiment, to whom special 'Rifle Barrelled Guns' had been issued, to replace the Rangers as guides through the forest, aided by the provincials."[12]

Captain Monypenny, in his journal, makes reference to the issue and practice with the "Rifled Guns."[13] But is this the first time that rifles were actually used? What about the Rangers in 1757?

Seventeen of these unique rifle balls have been recovered by Keith and Dan. One was found on Rogers' Island across the river from Fort Edward. Another was found along the route from the landing place to the battlesite of Lord Howe's skirmish. The remaining 15 were found on the site itself.

Musket balls: l-r: dropped ball, chewed ball; Brown Bess .75 caliber balls, various buckshot, French 60 caliber musket balls; rifled musket balls.

The finding of one of these balls on Rogers' Island and another along a route of travel might suggest that a rifle could have been carried by a Ranger. The reason the Rangers were camped on Rogers' Island was their dislike of British authority, which was returned. Since most British troops were encamped away from the Rangers, an argument, albeit weak, could be made that since the Rangers kept pretty much to themselves in camp, at least one Ranger had a rifle.

Robert Rogers and his Rangers were on the cutting edge of new tactics of warfare for English and American troops. His own "Rules of Ranging" set the standards of modern-day forces such as the Green Berets. If the Rangers were an elite unit of their time, and they most certainly were, then is it possible that they might have been issued a prototype of this new weapon to test out its competence, reliability and feasibility in forest warfare? Finally, it makes one wonder about the amount of rifled balls that were found dropped on the battlesite. Was it in the Lord Howe skirmish or the 1757 ambush on snowshoes? It would seem more probable that balls would be dropped from cold, frozen fingers in winter than on a hot day in summer.

All the hundreds of recovered musket balls, of both French and English origin, are drops (unfired musket balls); spent balls (deformed from hitting things such as human bone, flesh, trees, ice, or the ground itself); buckshot; split-shot; and chewed balls (deformed with teeth marks).

The "chewed balls" are especially interesting. One person suggested to me that perhaps this site was a temporary camp where the wounded from a battle might have been taken; and as field surgery was performed, the balls were placed in the soldier's mouth to help with the pain and keep from biting the tongue.

Another opinion was voiced that perhaps the finding of these chewed balls indicated a spot where soldiers were being punished or disciplined for infractions and were given a musket ball to chew on as they faced up to the lash.

In my opinion, this spot in the forest would not have been appropriate for either activity.

What I wholeheartedly agree with is the opinion of my late friend and fellow historian, Roger Dechame of Ticonderoga, who spent substantial time and research in his investigation of the "chewed ball" theory. Roger wrote an essay on this very subject, and I include some excerpts from it for the reader.

"The use of lead balls for soldiers to chew on during operations/amputations may have been done at some points, but was doubtful on most because of the following reasons: The diet of the 18th century soldier was sadly lacking in vitamins/minerals, etc., hence much scurvy, a disease rampant in the 18th century. The probability of wobbly teeth breaking, <u>and</u> being swallowed along <u>with</u> the ball, in the patient's gasps of pain, was considerable. More likely, to alleviate the pain and to keep the tongue from being swallowed, would be the use of a green piece of wood across the mouth, to bite into."[14]

Of the chewed bullets found, "most are not marked by front teeth but masticated by canines and molars. In soft lead, repeated mastication produces rugged asperity. Such dental jaw action, along with the bullet's velocity, will tear splinters when penetrating internal soft flesh, even in a superficial wound. A smooth, round bullet was less damaging, with the wound standing a better chance of healing."[15]

Montcalm wrote of the 1757 snowshoe ambush, and the use of chewed balls, in his diary of February 15, 1757, "We received news from Carillon. A few of our wounded are dying. Someone complained that the British used chewed bullets. It is a reproach that always turns up between nations at war."[16]

Coins

The carrying of money, at first glance, would have been more likely in the summer months, for various reasons. There would be more items carried that could be bartered for or sold and more of an opportunity to purchase them. Gambling was a favorite pastime in the eighteenth century, and a lot of idle hours would have been spent waiting for Fort Carillon to fall from a siege. Plus, the sheer quantity of coins found, apparently from thousands of soldiers of both sides, would tend to favor the location as the site of the skirmish between Langy's and Howe's forces in the summer of 1758. It would also be highly unlikely that coins would have been carried on a snowshoe scout/raid in the middle of winter. Not much reason for the use of such. So in using that thought process we tend to eliminate the possibility of the site being the 1757 snowshoe ambush…

Until one rereads Pvt. Thomas Brown's winter diary and recalls the words, "The next day, about 11 o'clock, I heard the shouts of Indians behind me, and I suppos'd they saw me; within a few minutes four came running down a mountain… they soon came up with me, took me by the neck and kiss'd me. On searching my pockets they found some money, which they were so fond of, that in trying who could get the most, they had like to have killed me."[17]

Medals

Two unidentified medals, apparently religious, were found at the site. One has a depiction of a Roman soldier's helmet upon it. Since the Roman Empire was throughout France and England, it could possibly have belonged to a soldier from either side. The second medal appears to depict a communion scene with an altar. This suggests to me that it might have belonged to someone of the Catholic faith.

Gun flints, coins and medals. Top left: British gun flint, top right: French gun flint. Bottom left: Roman helmet medallion; center: coins; bottom right: child on altar medallion.

Gun parts: Top: musket fore-end cap. Left: mainspring.
Right: frizzen. Bottom: sling swivel and barrel-band swivel.

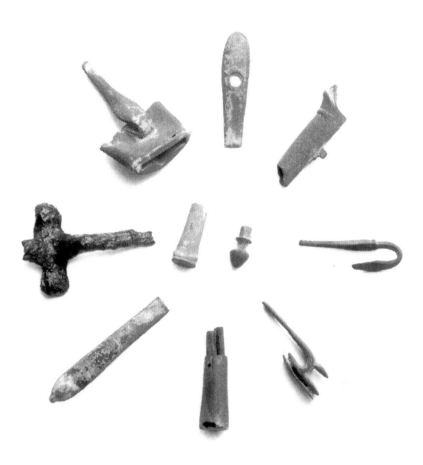

Various accoutrements. Clockwise from top: brass musket
furniture, ramrod keeper, bayonet scabbard frogs, ramrod tip
with remains of carved hickory rod, brass musket furniture,
iron sword frog, bayonet scabbard frog with attached
scabbard hilt (note triangular shape). Center: left, small
caliber ramrod tip; center right: bayonet scabbard brass stud.

Musket Parts and Locks

Of all the artifacts found, of both French and British origin, few convey more of a sense of the personalities of the original owners than the parts that remain from their weapons. When I look upon the pieces of the English locks, I wonder, could this be from the musket of Private Brown? "...fix'd myself behind a large pine, where I loaded and fir'd every opportunity; after I had discharged 6 or 7 times, there came a ball and cut off my gun just at the lock."[18] Or could it have been the musket that Lt. John Stark carried? "...but Stark, now having the command, and being almost the only Officer fit for duty, declared that he had a good position, and would fight the enemy until dark, and then retreat; that in such a course consisted their only safety; and that he would shoot the first man who fled. While speaking thus, a ball broke the lock of his gun; and, at the same moment, observing a Frenchman fall, he sprang forward, seized his gun, returned to his place, and continued the action."[19]

Top: Folding knife blade, folding knife with bone handle still
intact. Bottom: Tomahawk head and camp axe.

The Artifacts

Sources

1. Loescher, *History,* p. 334
2. Kemmer, p. 30
3. Knox, pp. 53-54
4. Gallup & Shaffer, pp. 66-67
5. Knox, p. 233
6. Bougainville, p. 81
7. Loescher, *History,* p. 279
8. Peterson, p. 131
9. Peterson, pp. 135-136
10. Peterson, p. 136
11. Hamilton, p. 217
12. Cuneo, p. 85
13. Monypenny, p. 348
14. Dechame
15. Ibid.
16. Montcalm, p. 154
17. Loescher, *History,* p. 333
18. Loescher, *History,* p. 332
19. Stark, p. 19

The Last Page

Okay. Here we have come to what is appropriately called "The Last Page." The facts have all been presented, the evidence and artifacts shown.

Here is where I leave you to choose: Is this location the scene of the battle on that cold, foggy day in January of 1757 when Robert Rogers and his Rangers, hurrying homeward in their flight from Lake Champlain, topped the crest of that small hill and came face to face with Charles-Michael de Langlade and his hidden force of French and Indians?

or

Is this the location of the scene of battle on that hot, sultry day in July of 1758 where Lord Howe led his scarlet regulars and provincial troops, blundering through the gloomy, primeval forest, only to lose his life to the French-led troops of Trépezec and Langy?

or

Was it the site of both?

Dan Blanchette and Keith Dolbeck at a site on Lake
Champlain with White's XLT metal detector.

Contributors

Keith Dolbeck

Keith has been a lifelong resident of Ticonderoga, New York, for fifty-plus years. He holds a B.S. degree in Science from Syracuse University and an M.S. from Cornell University. Mr. Dolbeck has been employed as an educator for the past 27 years, holding positions of associate professor and classroom teacher in college and high school. In addition, he has coached two high school varsity sports (softball and football) for the past 18 years.

Keith has always had an acute interest in local history with respect to the French and Indian and Revolutionary War periods. He has served as a lecturer at local schools and community sponsored programs. He is a trustee of the Ticonderoga Historical Society and a contributor to the Fort Ticonderoga Association.

Keith's interest in locating encampments and battlesites with the use of a metal locator has developed into a close association with the author of this book as well as many other authors on the subject of military history.

Daniel J. Blanchette

Dan was born in Hartford, Connecticut, and raised in Crown Point, New York, until the age of 16. He then moved to Ticonderoga, New York, where he graduated from Ticonderoga High School in 1988. He presently works for Essex County ARC as a Senior Residential Counselor.

Dan has always enjoyed local history, and was recently appointed Town Historian of Ticonderoga. He is very involved in making school presentations to young children to teach them about their historic town. He and his wife, Penny, have three sons: Zach, Danny and Ethan Alan.

Al Cederstrom, Photographer

Al received his B.S. in Marine Engineering from the Maine Maritime Academy, served two years in the U.S. Navy and then earned his M.Ed. in Science. He taught Math and Biology from 1956 to 1983.

Al lives in Queensbury, New York, and has been a freelance photographer since 1972. His photographs have appeared in *Adirondack Life, Down East Magazine and Calendar, New York Alive!, New York Sportsman, New York Conservationist* and other magazines; the *New York Times, Boston Globe, Hartford Courant, Glens Falls Post Star* and other newspapers; and several books, including *The Battle on Snowshoes*.

George "Peskunck" Larrabee

Peskunck is a special features contributor for *Muzzleloader* magazine. He also has written articles for the NMLRA's *Muzzle Blasts* magazine as well as the Dixie Gun Works' *Blackpowder Annual*. For several years he was Historical Editor of the *Black Powder Times*. In 1990 he was adopted into the Abenaki nation in Vermont. He is also a member of the Seven Indian Nations living history association, and serves as the Olawigha (scribe) of a specifically Abenaki living history group, Capitaine Jean Joseph's Band of Abenaki Warriors.

George C. Neumann, Foreword

Mr. Neumann is a well-known military historian whose accomplishments are many. A retired businessman, he held high positions in some of this country's most recognized companies. He was educated at Wesleyan and Princeton Universities and Harvard Business School. But he is best known as an authority on the American Revolution and the weapons used during that period.

He has served on the Advisory Boards of the Museum of Our National Heritage and the Valley Forge Historical Society; was a consultant and participant in the PBS Revolutionary War production, "Liberty"; has lectured at the Smithsonian, West Point, Valley Forge and many key Bicentennial battle re-enactments; received the Man at Arms Annual Cup Award, *Man at Arms* magazine; created the "Neumann Collection" of Revolutionary War Militaria now displayed at the Valley Forge National Historical Park; received the Distinguished Service Award and served on the Board of Directors and as a Fellow of the Company of Military Historians; and served as National Commander of the Brigade of the American Revolution.

Mr. Neumann is the author of:

The History of Weapons of the American Revolution, Harper & Row, 1967. Reprinted 1975.

Swords & Blades of the American Revolution, Stackpole, 1973. Reprinted 1979 and 1991.

The Collector's Illustrated Encyclopedia of the American Revolution, Co-Authored with Frank Kravic, Stackpole, 1975. Reprinted 1979, 1990, and 1997.

Early American Antique Country Furnishings, McGraw-Hill, 1984. Reprinted 1988 and 1993.

Battle Weapons of the American Revolution, Scurlock Publishing, 1998.

Joe Lee, Illustrator

Readers will recognize Joe's historically accurate and lively style, which has enlivened the interpretive displays at many historical sites and has graced the pages of several publications. His illustrations have appeared in the following books: *The Battle on Snowshoes* by Bob Bearor, *La Marine: The French Colonial Soldier in Canada, 1745-1761* by Andrew Gallup and Donald Shaffer, *Memoir of a French and Indian War Soldier* and *Sketch of the Virginia Soldier in the Revolution* by Andrew Gallup, *Freemen, Freeholders and Citizen Soldiers* and *Redcoats, Yankees and Allies* by Brenton Kemmer (all published by Heritage Books, Inc.); *Siege - 1759* by Brian L. Dunnigan, *Uniforms and Equipment of the United States Forces in the War of 1812* by Rene Chartrand (both published by the Old Fort Niagara Association); *Historic Colonial French Dress* by Judy Forbes (published by Smoke and Fire News); *Indian Clothing of the Great Lakes 1740-1840* by Sheryl Hartman, *America's First, First World War* by Timothy J. Todish (both published by Eagle's View Publishing); *Soldiers at the Straits* by Harry Burgess (published in Port Huron, Michigan) and *Fort St. Joseph in Port Huron* by Rosaline and Harry Burgess (published by Museum Press, Port Huron, Michigan). Joe and Darlene Lee, with Linda and William Knapp have published two books, *Whatcha-ma-call-its* and *Thinga-ma-jigs,* which they have sold to a publishing company in Charlotte, Michigan.

Bob Bearor (facing camera), Greg Geiger and Fred Gowen's dog, Sammy, enjoying a primitive canoe trip on South Bay. Photo by Fred Gowen.

❧ *Bibliography* ❧

Bearor, Bob. *The Battle on Snowshoes.* Bowie, Maryland: Heritage Books, Inc., 1997.

Bearor, Bob. "Langy, The Best There Ever Was." *Muzzle Blasts,* Vol. 56, No. 2, Oct. 1994.

Bougainville, Louis Antoine de. *Adventure in the Wilderness.* Edward P. Hamilton, editor and translator. Norman: University of Oklahoma Press, 1964.

Bourlamaque, Francois Charles de. *Letters de M. de Bourlamaque au Chevalier de Levis.* Quebec, Canada: Demers & Frere, 1891.

Burnham, Koert DuBois. *La Corne St. Luc - His Flame.* Northern New York American-Canadian Genealogical Society, 1991.

Cleaveland, Reverend John. Journal. *Bulletin of the Fort Ticonderoga Museum,* Vol. X, No. 3, 1959. Fort Ticonderoga, N.Y.

Costain, Thomas B. *The White and the Gold.* New York: Doubleday and Company, 1954.

Cuneo, John R. *Robert Rogers of the Rangers.* Fort Ticonderoga Museum, 1988. Ticonderoga, N.Y.

Day, Gordon M. "Rogers' Raid in Indian Tradition." *Historical New Hampshire.* 1982.

Dechame, Roger. "To Bite the Bullet." with Dr. Karl J. Bowers. Privately Printed, Ticonderoga, N.Y., 1994.

Dictionary of Canadian Biography (DCB) 15 vols. Toronto: University of Toronto Press. 1966-1991.

Gallup, Andrew, and Donald Shaffer. _La Marine: The French Colonial Soldier in Canada, 1745-1761._ Bowie, Maryland: Heritage Books, Inc. 1992.

Hamilton, Edward P. _The French and Indian Wars._ Garden City, N.Y.: Doubleday and Company, 1962.

Kemmer, Brenton C. _Freemen, Freeholders and Citizen Soldiers._ Bowie, Maryland: Heritage Books, Inc., 1997.

Knox, Captain John. _The Siege of Quebec._ Edited by Brian Connell. Mississauga, Ontario: Pendragon House Ltd.

Kopperman, Paul E. _Braddock at the Monongahela._ Pittsburgh: University of Pittsburgh Press. 1977.

Lewis, Meriwether Liston. _Montcalm, The Marvelous Marquis._ Vantage Press, 1961.

Loescher, Burt G. _History of Rogers Rangers._ Privately printed. San Mateo, California: 1946.

Loescher, Burt G. _Rogers Rangers: Genesis. The First Green Berets._ Privately printed. San Mateo, California: 1969.

Lucier, Armand Francis. _French and Indian War Notices Abstracted from Colonial Newspapers._ Vol. 3. Bowie, Maryland: Heritage Books, Inc., 1999.

Monypenny, Alexander. "The Monypenny Orderly Book," *The Bulletin of the Fort Ticonderoga Museum*, Vol. XII, No. 5-6, 1969; Vol. XIII, No. 1-2, 1971.

New York State Historical Association. *Proceedings*. Vol. X. Glens Falls, N.Y.: Glens Falls Publishing Company, 1910.

O'Callaghan, E.B., editor. *Documents Relating to the Colonial History of the State of New York*. 15 vols. Albany: Weed and Parsons, 1858.

Parkman, Francis. *Montcalm and Wolfe*. New York: Collier Books, 1962.

Peterson, Harold L. *The Treasury of the Gun*. New York: Ridge Press/Golden Press, 1962.

Pouchot, Pierre. *Memoirs on the Late War in North America Between France and England*. Translated by Michael Cardy, edited by Brian Leigh Dunnigan. Old Fort Niagara Association, Inc., 1994.

Richards, Frederick B. *The Black Watch at Ticonderoga and Major Duncan Campbell of Inverawe*. (1911) Reprinted, Bowie, Maryland: Heritage Books, Inc., 1999.

Roby, Luther. *Reminiscences of the French War, Robert Rogers' Journal, and A Memoir of General Stark*. (1831) Freedom, New Hampshire: Freedom Historical Society, 1988.

Rutledge, Joseph L. *Century of Conflict*. New York: Doubleday, 1956.

Slocum, Charles Elihu. *History of the Maumee River Basin from the Earliest Account to its Organization into Counties*. Privately printed. Defiance, Ohio: 1905. Reprinted, Bowie, Maryland: Heritage Books, Inc., 1997.

Society of Colonial Wars in the State of New York.
   Publication #49, Nov. 1942. New Haven, Connecticut:
   Tuttle, Morehouse and Taylor Co.

Stark, Caleb. *Memoir and Official Correspondence of General John
   Stark, with Notices of Several Other Officers of the Revolution.
   Also, a Biography of Capt. Phinehas Stevens, and of Col. Robert
   Rogers, with an Account of His Services in America during the
   "Seven Years' War."* (1877) Reprinted, Bowie, Maryland:
   Heritage Books, Inc., 1999.

Steele, Ian K. *Betrayals: Fort William Henry & the "Massacre."*
   New York: Oxford University Press, 1990.

⚜ Index ⚜

ABERCROMBY, Maj Gen James
xxi 21 27 59 82 20 Decided
Upon *Coup De Musketrie*
Without Artillery 33
Defeated 34 63 65
ABERCROMBY'S ARMY,
Overwhelming Confidence
Of 24 Soul Expired With
Death Of Howe 32
ABERCROMBY'S ATTACK,
Launched 23 Superb
Spectacle Of 24
ADK, Adirondack Mountain
Club xi
ALBANY, 24 Howe's Body
Supposedly Taken To 34
Langy Reconnoiters Road To
22
AMERICAN REVOLUTION,
Rifles Used Before The 81
ARCHEOLOGY, And Large-
scale Development 51
Conventional Methods 51
On Private Property 51
Random Digging 50
ARQUEBUSES, First Prize
Shooting With 81
ARTIFACTS, Found At Site 49
55 73 74 Ability To Identify
53 Condition, Noted 52
Depth Of, Noted 52
Identification Of 52

ARTIFACTS (cont.)
Iron, Care Of 53 Metal And
Non-metallic 52 Pewter,
Care Of 53 Placement Of,
Noted 53 Position In
Ground, Noted 53 Silver,
Care Of 53 Type Of Sod,
Noted 53
ARTILLERY, Transported For
Abercromby's Attack 23
AXE, Belt, Found At Battlesite
74 Rifleman's, Found At
Battlesite 74
BAKER, Robert 80 Wounded In
Ambush 12 Taken Captive
13
BALD MOUNTAIN, Also
Called Mont Pélée And
Rogers' Rock 25
BASSERODE, Capt De,
Marches Out To Ambush
Rangers In 1757 9
BATEAUX, In Abercromby's
Attack 23
BATTLE OF LA BARBUE
CREEK, xxi
BATTLE OF QUEBEC, xxi
BATTLE ON SNOWSHOES
(1758), xxi 43 22 50 56 58 66
Ballad xi
BATTLE ON SNOWSHOES,
1758 (book) xi xv 42

BATTLES, Accounts Of 55
BATTLESITE (1757),
  Descriptions Of 57-58
BATTLESITE (1758), Accounts
  Of 65 Traditional Belief Of
  Location Of 64 Various
  Descriptions Of 65-66
  Visited By Jefferson And
  Madison 64
BATTLESITES, Descriptions In
  Diaries And Letters 41
  Determining Location Of 41
  Documented With Use Of
  Metal Detectors 51 Locations
  Determined By Reenactment
  Methods 42 Other Locations
  Disproved 42
BAYONET FRAGMENT,
  Found At Battlesite 74
BAYONET SCABBARD
  FROGS, Found At Battlesite
  74
BAYONETS, Rangers Killed By
  10
BEAR MOUNTAIN, 57 68-69
BEARN REGIMENT, 25
BEAROR, Becky iii xv Bob ix-x
  xiii 98-99 Cliff iii xv 35 48
  Holly xi xv 35 48 99 Jenny iii
  xv Ted iii xv Terri 35
BEAUJEAU, Daniel De 68
BELLICO, Russell xii
BERNES RIVER, 65
BERNETZ, Chevalier De 65
BERNETZ RIVER, 65-66 69
  (Trout Brook) 30
BIGOT, Failed To Provide
  Supplies For Montcalm's
  Army 33
BLACK POWDER, 45 47
BLACK WATCH HIGHLAND
  REGIMENT, Casualties Of
  33-34

BLANCHARD, Martha 42
BLANCHETTE, Daniel J x xii
  xix-xx 42 49 74 82 96 Danny
  96 Ethan Alan 96 Penny 96
  Zach 96
BOLTON, Reginald P 53
*BOOK OF BUCKSKINNING
  VII,* 48
BOUGAINVILLE, Louis
  Antoine De 22 23 67 80
  Account Of 1758 Battle 65
  Comments On Death Of
  Howe 33 Description Of
  Mohawk Trail 66 Journal
  Account Of Sleigh Ambush
  55 Mentions Destruction Of
  Bridge 63 Recorded Langy's
  Sighting Of Abercromby's
  Advance Guard 24
BOURLAMAQUE, Charles
  Francois De xxi 23 Orders
  French Troops To Destroy
  Bridges 25 Retreat And
  Destruction Of Bridge 63
BRADDOCK'S DEFEAT, On
  The Monongahela 7 20 24 68
BRADSTREET, Col 24
  Reconnoitered Landing
  Place 25
BRAY, George xii xvi
BREWER, Ensign, With Rogers
  In January 1757 1
BRIDGES, Destroyed By French
  63-64 Destruction Caused
  British To March Over Land
  64
BRIGADE OF THE
  AMERICAN
  REVOLUTION, 97
BRITISH, Dislike For Rangers
  84
BRODERICK, Dan xv 45
BROWN, Private Thomas 15 45

BROWN, Private Thomas
(cont.)
79-80 86 90 Description Of
1757 Battlesite Location 57-
58 Description Of Distance
To 1757 Battlesite 56 Diary
Of 52 His Distance From
Ticonderoga After Sleigh
Ambush 55 Narrative Of 11-
14
BUCKLE, Cartridge Box, Found
At Battlesite 74 Shoulder
Strap, Found At Battlesite 74
BUCKLE FRAGMENTS, Found
At Battlesite 74
BUCKLES, Found At Battlesite,
73 79 Knee, 74 Shoe, Pairs 74
Small Equipment, 74
BUCKSHOT, Found At
Battlesite 81 84
BULKELEY, Lt, Commands
Relief Party 14
BULLETS, Found At Battlesite
81
BURGESS, Harry 98 Rosaline 98
BURNSIDE, Thomas 14
BURNT CAMP, Also Called
Countrecoeur 25
BUTTONS, Various, Found At
Battlesite 74
CALVER, William L 53
CANDLESTICK HOLDER,
Found At Battlesite 74
CAPE BRETON ISLAND, 20
CARILLON, 6 15 66-67
Distance From Sleigh
Ambush 55-56 French
Troops Depart Before Sleigh
Ambush 5 Garrison In
January 1757 4 Langy And
Trépezec Head For 30
Langy's Scouts Prior To
Abercromby's Attack On 22

CARILLON (cont.)
Montcalm At 24 Rangers
Camp Near, January 1757 2
Rumors Of Impending
Attack Against 22 Stevens
And Rangers Questioned At
23 (See Also Fort Carillon)
CARLSON, R 13 Roxanne xv
CARTRIDGE, Paper 47
CERTAINTY, Definition 41
CEDERSTROM, Al xvii 96
CHAMPLAIN VALLEY, 20
CHARTRAND, Rene 98
CHAUSSONS, Wool Slippers
For Lining Moccasins (illus.)
77
CHEWED BALLS, Caused
Severe Wounds 85 Found At
Battlesite 84 Possible
Explanations For 84-85
CHRISTIAN IV, King Of
Denmark, First To Equip
Troops With Rifles 81
CLEAVELAND, John, Account
Of 1758 Battle 65 Diary
Account Of Ambush Of
Rogers Near Fort Anne 60
Journal Account Of
Destruction Of Bridge 64
CLOTHING, Eighteenth
Century 42
COB (Silver Coinage), Found At
Battlesite 74
COINS, Found At Battlesite 49
86 Reasons For Carrying 85-
86
*COLLECTOR'S ILLUSTRATED
ENCYCLOPEDIA OF THE
AMERICAN REVOLUTION*,
(book) 53
COMPAGNIES FRANCHES,
With Langlade In 1757 7

COMPAGNIES FRANCHES
DEL LA MARINE, 6
COMPANY OF MILITARY
HISTORIANS, 97
COMPASS, Architectural,
Plotting Sites With 41
CONJECTURE, Definition 41
CONNECTICUT
PROVINCIALS, Great
Casualties Blamed On
Rogers 60
CONTESTS, Smoothbores
versus Rifles 81
CONTRECOEUR, Also Called
Burnt Camp 25
COOK'S MOUNTAIN, 67-68
COPPERS, King George, Found
At Battlesite 74
CROWN POINT, 2 11 20 (See
Fort St Frederic, St Frederic)
CUMBERFORT, Lt 31
CUNEO, 31 63
CUSTER, George Armstrong 68
D'ASTRAL, Lt, Marches Out To
Ambush Rangers In 1757 9
DAIUTE, Mark 45
DEAD SHOUT, 13
DECHAME, Roger xvii 85
DELANCEY, 80
DEROUILLY, 6 French Officer
In Sleigh Ambush 5
DIET, Of 18th-Century Soldiers,
Deficiencies Of 85
DISTANCE, From Fivemile
Point To Rangers' Campsite
44 From Rangers' Campsite
To La Chute 49
DIXON, Bonnie 42 Orley 42
DOLBECK, Anita xvi Keith x
xii xv xix-xx 42-43 49 54 68
74 82 95
DUNNIGAN, Brian L 98
DURANTAYE, xxi

EASTMAN, Ranger Private,
Statement About Rogers 4
EIGHTEENTH-CENTURY
GEAR, 43
EYRE, Maj, Grants Rogers 33
Men In January 1757 1
FATIGUE, As A Factor In
Combat 69
FINIAL BAYONET
SCABBARD TIPS, Found At
Battlesite 74
FIRE, Made With Flint And
Steel 48
FIRST BATTLE ON
SNOWSHOES, xxi
FITCH, Regiments Of, With
Rogers In Abercromby's
Attack 27
FIVEMILE CREEK, Difficulty
Of Traveling In Its Ravines
44 Rangers Ambush Sleighs
Near, January 1757 2
FIVEMILE POINT, 43 Sleigh
Ambush At, January 1757 6
Used As Reference To
Calculate Distance 55
FLATBOATS WITH
ARTILLERY, In
Abercromby's Attack 23
FLOTILLA, In Abercromby's
Attack, Completely Covered
The Lake 24
FORBES, Judy 98
FOREST, Near 1758 Battlesite,
Description 64
FORK, Found At Battlesite 74
FORT ANNE, Rangers Camped
Near Ruins Of 59 Rogers
Ambushed By Marin Near
60
FORT BEAUSEJOUR, 22
FORT BULL, 20
FORT CARILLON, 21 65 67 86

FORT CARILLON (cont.)
1758 Attack Planned 20
Distance From Sleigh
Ambush 55 (See Also
Carillon, Ticonderoga)
FORT CROWN POINT, See
Crown Point, St Frederic
FORT DECHARTRES, xi
FORT DUQUESNE, 68 1758
Attack Planned 20 Rifles
Issued In Expedition
Against 82 Rumors Of
Impending Attack Against
21
FORT EDWARD, xi 59 82
Langy Reconnoiters Road To
22 Rogers Scout From, In
January 1757 1
FORT FRONTENAC, Rumors
Of Impending Attack
Against 21
FORT LIGONIER, xi
FORT NECESSITY, xi
FORT NIAGARA, xi Rumors
Of Impending Attack
Against 21
FORT NUMBER FOUR, xi
FORT OSWEGO, 22 Fall Of 20
FORT ST FREDERIC, 6 1758
Attack Planned 20 21
Rangers Camp Near,
January 1757 2
FORT TICONDEROGA, xi xix
20 54 Annual War College
At 50 Grande Encampment
At 35 Staff Of xvi War
College At xii (See Also
Ticonderoga, Carillon)
FORT TICONDEROGA
ASSOCIATION, 95
FORT WESTERN, xi
FORT WILLIAM HENRY, xi
xxi 11-12 14 20 25 32 66

FORT WILLIAM HENRY
(cont.)
Attack And Siege Of 22
Ranger Scout Departs From
2 Rangers Head Toward,
After Sleigh Ambush 4 9
Revenge For Loss Of 24
Rogers At 1
FRENCH ROYAL HORSE
GUARDS, And Rifled
Carbines 81
FRIZZEN, Found At Battlesite
74
FRIZZEN FEATHER SPRING,
Found At Battlesite 74
FRIZZEN PAN, 47
FUSILS, French, Misfiring Of,
During Ambush 10
GAGE'S LIGHT INFANTRY,
Rifles Issued To 82
GAGE'S REGULARS, 59
GAITERS, (illus.) 76
GALLUP, Andrew 98
GAMBLING, In 18th Century
86
GANAOUSKE BAY,
(Northwest Bay) 66
GARDINER, Killed 10
GEIGER, Greg xii xv 35 99
GEORGE, King Of England 21
GIDDINGS, Capt 60
GOWEN, Fred xii xv 45 47-48
99
GRANVILLE, Capt, Marches
Out To Ambush Rangers In
1757 9
GRAPPINS, Ice Creepers (illus.)
78
GREEN, Anne xi
GREEN BERETS, Rogers Set
Standards For 84
GRIDS, Of Sites Where
Artifacts Were Found 53

GUESS, Definition 41
GUETRES, Gaiters (illus.) 77
GUN FLINTS, Found At
Battlesite 74
GUN FURNITURE, Brass,
Found At Battlesite 74
GUNS, Drying Of, After Sleigh
Ambush 5
HAMILTON, Edward P 65
Translation Of
Bougainville's Description
Of Mohawk Trail 66
HARTMAN, Sheryl 98
HATCHET, Square-poled,
Found At Battlesite 74
HEBECOURT, Capt De,
Description Of Battlesite
Location 56
HERRICK'S
REVOLUTIONARY
MILITIA, 96
HISTORICAL SIGN, Marking
Site Of Lord Howe's Death
65
*HISTORY OF THE LATE WAR
IN NORTH AMERICA AND
THE ISLANDS OF THE
WEST INDIES*, (book) 66
*HISTORY WRITTEN WITH
PICK AND SHOVEL*, (book)
53
HOBBS, Capt 80
HOBBS' COMPANY, 14
HOT BISCUIT DINER, 42
HOWE, Lord George Augustus
Viscount x xii xx xxi 21 27 33
52 55 61 64 65 67 80 82 86 93
And Stark Before
Abercromby's Attack 24
Controversy Regarding
Burial Of 34 Determining
Factor In Death Of 63 Joins
Rogers And Rangers 21

HOWE, Lord George Augustus
Viscount (cont.)
Killed 31-32 Reconnoitered
Landing Place 25 Stone
Found Near Village Of
Ticonderoga 34
ICE CREEPERS, (illus.) 78
Found At Battlesite 49 73-74
Proof Of Winter Battle 73
INDIAN, "La Demoiselle"
(Unemakemi, "Old Britain")
Killed At Pickawillany 7
INDIANS, Reasons For
Abandoning French Before
1758 Battle 67-68
IRWIN, William 59
JAEGER STYLE RIFLES, 82
JEFFERSON, Thomas, Visited
Lord Howe Site 64
KEMMER, Brenton 98
KENNEDY, Lt 9 57 Killed 10 14
Samuel With Rogers In
January 1757 1
KILBY, 80
KNAPP, Linda 98 William 98
KNIFE BLADE, Found At
Battlesite 74
KNIVES, Found At Site 49
KNOX, John 80
KRAVIC, Frank J 53
LA CHUTE RIVER, 20 25 30 48
64 67 69
LA CORNE, St Luc De,
Devastating Ambush 59
LA PETITE GUERRE, 7 22
LA REINE REGIMENT, 56
With Langlade In 1757 7
LAKE CHAMPLAIN, 1-2 20 23
66-67 93 Frozen 11 Rogers
Description Of Camp Near
56 Shore Where Rogers
Ambushed Sleighs 43 Sleigh
Ambush On Ice On 5

LAKE GEORGE, xvi 1-2 14 66-67 (Lake St Sacrement) 23 Ranger Scouts In 1758 23 Rogers Route Of Retreat To 60-61
LAKE GEORGE BASIN LAND CONSERVANCY, xvi
LAKE GEORGE HISTORICAL ASSOCIATION, xvi
LAKE ST SACREMENT, (Lake George) 23
LANGIS, (Also Langy) 22 Sieur De 23
LANGIS DE MONTEGRON, (Also Langy) Jean Baptiste Levreault 22
LANGLADE, Charles-Michel Mouet De 9 80 93 Ambushes Rogers In 1757 10 At Braddock's Defeat 7 Sent To Ambush Rangers 6 Expert In *La Petite Guerre* 7
LANGUEDOC, Regiment With Langlade In 1757 7
LANGY, (Also Langis) xxi 22 24 35 67-69 86 93 And 1758 Battle On Snowshoes 56 And Detachment Get Lost In Woods 30 And Trépezec Clash With Rogers 30 And Trépezec Lost In The Woods, Comments 66 Defeats Rogers In 1758 Battle On Snowshoes 58 Detached To Mont Pélée 25 Dispatched To Warn Vaudreuil 23 In Command Of Detachment 23 Lost For 12 Hours 65 Might Have Shot Howe 32 Scouts In 1758 22 Surrounds Stevens And Rangers In 1758 23 Warns Montcalm 23

LANGY, (cont.) Watched Abercromby's Flotilla Advance 24 Wounded 32
LANGY DE MONTEGRON, (Also Langis) Ambushed Rogers In 1760 43
LAPANN, Carroll xi Fred xi xvii
LARRABEE, George "Flintlock" 96 George "Peskunck" xvi 96
LEE, Darlene 98 Joe 97
LEMOYNE, Catherine iii Charles iii
LES ARBRES MATACHES, 66
LEVIS, Chevalier De xxi 66
LIVE SHOUT, 13
LOESCHER, Burt G xvi
LONGEE, (Langis, Langy) 22
LORD HOWE SKIRMISH, 50
LORD HOWE STREET, In Village Of Ticonderoga 65
LOUISBOURG, 1758 Attack Planned 20 Rumors Of Impending Attack Against 21
LUSIGNAN, Paul Louis, Commandant At Carillon In 1757 4 Told Of Sleigh Ambush 6
LYMAN, Regiments Of, With Rogers In Abercromby's Attack 27
MACDONALD, Grace xvi
MACHAULT, (ship) 79
MADISON, James, Visited Lord Howe Site 64
MANTE, Thomas, Laments Death Of Howe 32
MAP, In Mante's History 66 Sketch Of The Country Round Tyconderoga 26 Marquis of Sligo 28-29

MAP, (cont.)
Topographical, Plotting Sites
With 41
MARIN, Joseph, Ambushed
Rogers Near Fort Anne 59
MATCHLOCK, Snapping 81
MAXIMILIAN I, 81
MAZZEO, Marilyn xvi Mario
xvi
MEDALS, Found At Battlesite
74 86
METAL DETECTING,
Archeological 49
Archeologically Acceptable
Methods 51 Establishment
Of Search Area 52
Identification And
Cataloging Of Artifacts 52
Methodology 51-53
Photographing The Search
Area 53 Preservation Of
Artifacts 53 Sources
Consulted 53
METAL DETECTORS, xii xix 49
51
MOCCASINS, Center-seam
(illus.) 75 High-top (illus.) 77
Indian Shoes 79 Liners For
(illus.) 77
MOHAWK TRAIL, 66
MONONGAHELA, Braddock's
Defeat At The 20 24
MONRO, Col xxi
MONT PÉLÉE, 35 67-68 Also
Called Bald Mountain And
Rogers' Rock 25 Trépezec
And Langy Ordered To 30
MONTCALM, Marquis De xxi
22 25 69 85 Awaiting
Reinforcements 27 Builds
Abatis 33 Defeat Of
Abercromby 34 65 Retreat &
Destruction Of Bridge 63

MONTCALM, Marquis De
(cont.)
Told Of Abercromby's
Approach 24 Trépezec 's
Orders From 68 Warned By
Langy 23
MONTCALM'S ARMY, 66
MONTREAL, xi 20 Langy Sent
To 23
MONYPENNY, Capt, Orderly
Book Of 52 Reference To
Rifles By 82
MULLIGAN, Robert xii
MUSEUM OF OUR
NATIONAL HERITAGE, 97
MUSKET BALLS, Found at
Battlesite, 49 74 Chewed, 81
Drops 84 Rifled 81 Spent
Balls 84
MUSKET PARTS AND LOCKS,
Found At Battlesite 90
MUSKET SIGHT, Found At
Battlesite 74
MUSKETS, 42 Drying Of, By
Rangers 56 Procedure For
Drying 45 (illus.) 46
NATIVE AMERICAN
WOODLAND COMPACT,
96
NEUMANN, George C x xii xvi
53 97
NEUMANN COLLECTION OF
REVOLUTIONARY WAR
MILITARIA, 97
NIAGARA, xxi
NIPES, Liners For Moccasins
(illus.) 77
NORTHWEST BAY,
(Ganaouske Bay) 66
"OLD BRITAIN", 7
OLD FORT NIAGARA
ASSOCIATION, 98

OPERATIONS/
AMPUTATIONS, 85
OPINION, Definition 41
OX SHOE, Half, Found At
Battlesite 74
PAGE, Caleb, Killed 14 With
Rogers In January 1757 1
PARKMAN, 32 Francis 21
William Great Uncle Of
Francis 21
PELL-DECHAME, Stephanie
xvii
PENCIL, Found At Battlesite 74
PICKAWILLANY, Destroyed
By Langlade And Pontiac 7
PINEY, Henry, shot French
Officer Who Killed Howe 32
PITT, Prime Minister William
20 21
PLAINS OF ABRAHAM, xxi
POCKET KNIFE, Found At
Battlesite 74
PONTIAC, Ottawa War Chief 7
POUCHOT, Capt Pierre xxi 59
Comments On Death Of
Howe 32
POWDER CHARGE, Wet,
Removal Of 47
PRISONERS, French 11 Caught
In 1757 Sleigh Ambush 4
PUTNAM, Maj Israel, Taken
Prisoner 59 Ambushed By
Marin 60
QUEBEC, Rumors Of
Impending Attack 21
RAMROD, 47
RAMROD GUIDE, Found At
Battlesite 74
RAMROD TIPS, Found At
Battlesite 74
RANGERS, 80 93 Ambushed
After Rogers' Marksmanship
Duel 59

RANGERS (cont.)
And 1757 Sleigh Ambush 4
Beaten By Langis 22
Decimated In 1758 Battle On
Snowshoes 66 Dislike Of
British Authority 84 Dry
Their Muskets 9 Flee From
Ambush 11 Howe Killed At
Head Of 31 Joined By Howe
21 Likely Had Rifles 82 84
Need To Dry Guns After
Sleigh Ambush 5 On Cutting
Edge Of Tactics Of Warfare
84 Ordered Forward To
Reconnoiter 25 Possible 1757
Campsite 44 48 Reasons
Why They Did Not Travel In
Fivemile Creek Ravines 44
Retreat After Ambush 14
Return To Campsite To Dry
Muskets 45 Route Of Travel
43 Scout Of January 1757 1-2
Scouting Lake George And
South Bay In 1758 23 Sleigh
Ambush In January 1757 6
Surrounded By Langy In
1758 23 Type Of Moccasins
Favored By (illus.) 77
RAQUETTES (SNOWSHOES),
43 48 French Troops' Lack
Of 11 Langlade Equipped
With 7
RATIONS, Scant 69
RAVINES, Of Fivemile Creek,
Difficulty Of Traveling In 44
REENACTORS, Around
Ticonderoga 42
RELIC HUNTING, 49
RESEARCH, xii
RIFLE BALLS, Found At
Battlesite 82 84 Found
Between Landing Place And
Battlesite 82

RIFLE BALLS, (cont.)
Found On Rogers' Island 82
RIFLES, American 82 Early Use
Of 81 Jaeger Style 82
Kentucky/Pennsylvania 82
Use During French And
Indian War 82
ROGERS, Robert, x xx xxi 11-12
24 93 After Action Reports
52 Ambushed By Langlade
In 1757 10 Ambushed By
Marin After Shooting At
Marks 59-60 Ambushed In
1760 By Langy 43 Ambushes
Sleighs In January 1757 2
And Destruction Of St
Francis Indian Village 59
And Rangers Ordered
Forward To Reconnoiter 25
And Sleigh Ambush 43
Beaten By Langy 22 Became
Lost In The Woods Prior To
Abercromby's Attack 27
Breaks Ranger Rule 4
Captures Sleighs And
Prisoners 4 Clashes With
Langy And Trépezec 30
Defeated By Langy In 1758
Battle On Snowshoes 58
Description Of 1757
Battlesite Location 57-58
Description Of Distance To
1757 Battlesite 56 Erroneous
Facts And Figures In Many
Reports 60 Flees From
Ambush 11 Forty Of His
Men Killed In Marin's
Ambush 60 Gave Orders To
Dry Guns 45 Had A Lot On
His Mind At Time Of 1757
Battle 56 Incorrect Report Of
1758 Battle On Snowshoes
58

ROGERS, Robert, (cont.)
Incorrect Report Of St
Francis Massacre 59 Joined
By Howe 21 Journal
Account Of 1757 Battlesite
56 Laments Death Of Howe
32 Langy Was Every Bit His
Equal 66 Legendary
Scouting And Cockiness 5
Mistaken Perception Of
West Direction 58 Never
Mentioned Firing At Marks
Before Ambush 60 On
Cutting Edge Of Tactics Of
Warfare 84 On Scout In
January 1757 1 Orders Men
To Kill Prisoners If Attacked
9 Possible Musket-drying
Site 48 Reconnoitered
Landing Place 25 Reluctance
To Tell All The Facts 59
Reports Not Always
Truthful 58 Retreats After
Ambush 14 Wounded In
Forehead 10 57
ROGERS, James, With Brother
Robert In January 1757 1
ROGERS' ISLAND, Rifle Ball
Found On 82 84
ROGERS' RANGERS, xii And
1758 Battle On Snowshoes
56 See Also Rangers; Rogers
ROGERS' ROCK, 67 xvi Also
Called Bald Mountain And
Mont Pélée 25
ROUSSILLON, Regiment With
Langlade In 1757 7
ROUTE DES AGNIERS, 66
(Mohawk Trail) 6
ROYAL ROUSSILLON,
Battallion 65
SABBATH DAY POINT,
Abercromby's Armada At 24

ST FREDERIC, Garrison In January 1757 4 Rumors Of Impending Attack Against 22 Sleighs Ambushed On Way To 5 See Also Fort St Frederic, Crown Point

ST HELEN'S ISLAND, xi

ST MARY'S CEMETERY, Traditionally Believed Near 1758 Battlesite 65

ST PETER'S EPISCOPAL CHURCH, Howe Supposedly Buried In 34

SAMMY THE DOG, 99

SCURVY, Rampant In 18th Century 85

SENTRIES, Ranger, At Gun Drying Site 45

SHAFFER, Donald 98

SHAW, Chris xi

SHOE BUCKLES, Found At Site 49

SHOES, (illus.) 75 Center-seam Moccasin (illus.) 75 Double-soled (illus.) 75 Found At Battlesite 79 Single-soled (illus.) 75 versus Moccasins 80

SHUTES, Ranger Private, Statement About Rogers 4

SITES, Alleged "Documented" 50

SLEIGH AMBUSH, By Rogers In 1757 4 Described By Thomas Brown 11-12 French Escort In 5

SLING BAND, Found At Battlesite 74

SMALLER SNOWSHOE BATTLE, xxi

SMOKE AND FIRE NEWS, 98

SMOOTHBORES, versus Rifles 81

SNOW, Waist-deep During Sleigh Ambush In 1757 4

SNOWSHOE AMBUSH, Possible Use Of Chewed Balls In 85

SNOWSHOES *(Raquettes),* xii 42 60-61 79-80 Langlade Equipped With 7 French Regulars Not Equipped With 9

SOULIERS DE CHEVREUIL, High-top Moccasins (illus.) 77

SOUTH BAY, Ranger Scouts In 1758 23

SPEAKMAN, Capt Thomas 9 57 80 And 1757 Sleigh Ambush 2 Captures Sleighs And Prisoners 4 With Rogers In January 1757 1

SPIKEMAN, Capt, Dead 14 Killed 13 Wounded In Ambush 12

SPLIT SHOT, Found At Battlesite 81 84

SPOONS AND SPOON FRAGMENTS, Found At Battlesite 74

STARK, John, 9 14 57 90 And 1757 Sleigh Ambush 2 43 And Howe Before Abercromby's Attack 24 Assists Rogers During Ambush 10 Kills Indian On Boulder 11 With Rogers In January 1757 1

STEVENS, Simon, Surrounded By Langy In 1758 23

STOCK, Brass Repair For, Found At Battlesite 74

STONE, Lord Howe, Found Near Village Of Ticonderoga 34

SWIVELS, Sling, Found At
Battlesite 74
TECHNOLOGY, Its Use To
Locate Historical Sites 50-51
THAW, Of January 1757 43
TICONDEROGA, xxi 2 20 24 64
85 Brown's Distance From,
After Sleigh Ambush 55
Village Of 19-20 Village Of,
Lord Howe Stone Found
Near 34 Weakness Of 33
TICONDEROGA CREEK, 65
TICONDEROGA HISTORICAL
SOCIETY, 95
TIONDEROGA
(TICONDEROGA), 11-12 14
TODISH, Timothy J 98
TOMAHAWKS, 57 Found At
Site 49
TOW, 47
TRACY, Lt, Taken Prisoner 59
TREKKING, xii
TRÉPEZEC , 35 67-69 93 And
Langy Lost In The Woods,
Comments 66 Might Have
Shot Howe 32 Mortally
Wounded 32 Sent To Mont
Pélée With Langy 25 What
Sort Of A Man Was He 68
TROUT BROOK, 19-20 27 34
48-49 67-68 (Bernetz River)
30 Different Names Of 65

TROUT BROOK VALLEY, xii
xxi 43 58 60 66
VALLEY FORGE HISTORICAL
SOCIETY, 97
VAUDREUIL, Gov, Failed To
Provide Men For
Montcalm's Army 33
Warned By Langy 23
VERMONT, 43
VITAMINS/MINERALS,
Lacking In 18th Century
Diet 85
WADDING, 47
WAR COLLEGE, Annual, At
Fort Ticonderoga 50
WASHINGTON, George, And
Braddock At The
Monongahela 24
WATER, Lack Of Fresh 69
WEATHER CONDITIONS, 43
WELLER, Dick xi xvii June xi
WHALEBOATS, In
Abercromby's Attack 23
WHITE'S ELECTONIC
SPECTRUM MODEL XLT
METAL DETECTOR, 51
WOLFE, Gen James xxi 20-21
WOOD CREEK, Rogers
Ambushed By Marin 59-60
WORM, 47
WOUNDED MEN, Abandoned
After 1757 Battle 57

Made in the USA
Charleston, SC
06 August 2013